LOL CAT
BIBLE

LOL CAT BIBLE

In teh beginnin Ceiling Cat maded teh Skiez an da Erfs n stuffs

Martin Grondin

Ulysses Press

Published in the United States by
ULYSSES PRESS
P.O. Box 3440
Berkeley, CA 94703
www.ulyssespress.com

ISBN: 978-1-56975-734-5
Library of Congress Control Number 2009930129

Printed in Korea by Tara TPS through Four Colour Print Group

10 9 8 7 6 5 4 3 2 1

Acquisitions Editor: Kelly Reed
Managing Editor: Claire Chun
Proofreader: Lauren Harrison
Design: what!design @ whatweb.com
Production: what!design @ whatweb.com, Judith Metzener

Distributed by Publishers Group West

PUBLISHER'S NOTE

This book is a parody that was created in cooperation with the LOLCat Bible Translation Project (www.lolcatbible.com), a Wiki that accepts contributions from users under the GNU Free Documentation License. The author and publisher reserve all available rights in the book as published subject to the terms of the foregoing license.

The photographs in this book were submitted to the publisher by various individuals who assured us in signed releases that they took and own the photos, control all rights in the photos, and are empowered to grant permission to us for use of the photos.

Contents

Ceiling Cat Maek Awl teh Stuffz

Genesis 1

1 Oh hai! In teh beginnin Ceiling Cat maded teh skys an teh Urfs, but he no eated dem.

2 Teh Urfs no has shayps an has darwk fase, an Ceiling Cat roed invisible bike ovah teh wawters.

3 At furst, no has lyte. An Ceiling Cat sez, "I can has lite?" An lite wuz. **4** An Ceiling Cat sawed teh lite, to see stuffs, an splitted teh lite frum teh dark, but dat wuz OK cuz kittehs can has site in teh dark an not fallz ovah nethin. **5** An Ceiling Cat sez, "Teh lite be Day an teh dark Nite. Dat wuz teh nawt secund day!

6 An Ceiling Cat sez, "Iz in ur wawters, makin a ceiling." An he maded a hole in teh ceiling. **7** An Ceiling Cat did teh skys wif wawters down an wif wawters up. It happun. **8** An Ceiling Cat sez, "I can has teh firmmint (wich is funnee Bibel naem fer ceiling)?" An dis wuz teh nawt furst day!

9 An Ceiling Cat got awl teh wawters in ur base, an Ceiling Cat maed drie plase cus kittehs DO NOT WANT wet. **10** An Ceiling Cat called teh drie plase teh floor and wawters teh baf tub. An it wuz gud.

11 An Ceiling Cat sez, "Iz gunna maek sum grass so kittehs can barf on teh floor." So der wuz seedz an stuffs, an fruitzors an vegbatels. An a corm. It happun. **12** An Ceiling Cat awlso maek green dings wif big leefs, so kittehs can chew on dem. **13** An dat wuz teh fird day, an Ceiling Cat do jazzhands.

14 An Ceiling Cat sez, "I can has lites in teh skys fer splittin day an nite?" **15** It happun, lites everywhar, liek Crismus, srsly. **16** An Ceiling Cat did two grate big lites, teh most big fer day, teh othah fer nite. **17** An Ceiling Cat screw dem on teh ceiling, wif big nails an stuff, to lite teh Urfs.

18 An dey rule teh day an teh nite. Ceiling Cat see. Is gud. **19** Dat wuz teh forf day, and Ceiling Cat go, "W00t!"

20 An Ceiling Cat sez, "Wawers gif me fishies, an teh ceiling gif me burds, so kittehs can noms dem." But Ceiling Cat no eated dem. **21** An Ceiling Cat maed big fishies an baf tub monstahs, wich wuz big liek moo-cows, but dey no moo, onlee eet kittehs. An he maek othah stuffs dat moev, an Ceiling Cat see dat it wuz gud. **22** An Ceiling Cat sez "Oh hai, maek bebehs, kthx. An dunt worree Iz no wach yu secksy, iz not dat kind uv kitteh." **23** An dat wuz teh fif day.

24 An Ceiling Cat sez, "I can has moar livin stuffs, moo-cows, creepy tings, an othah aminals?" It happun. **25** An Ceiling Cat did moar livin stuffs, moo-cows, creepy tings, an othah aminals, an he no eated dem.

26 An Ceiling Cat sez, "Let us maek peopul kind ov liek us, cuz we so cyoot. An dey gunna cleen teh howses an bring teh fud. Dey also haf fumbs to opun teh can openers."

27 So Ceiling Cat maed teh peopul dat wuz kind ov liek him, an dey can has can openers. He maed dem, man an wimun.

28 An Ceiling Cat sez to dem, "Oh hai! Maek bebehs ok? An pwn teh baf tub, an teh floors, an teh moo-cows. Kthnx."

29 An Ceiling Cat sez, "Luk! Teh Urfs, I has it. I no gunna nom it. Dey fer yu to eet! **30** Awl teh moo-cows an burdies, yu can has teh green leefs to nom."

31 An Ceiling Cat sez, "W00t! It gud enuf fer relees as vershun 0.8a. Kthxbai."

Genesis 2

1 Teh ceiling an teh floors wer awl dun. Awl teh stuffs in dem wer dun too, an Ceiling Cat was liek, "Iz awl tired an stuff. Iz taek naps."
2 On teh sevunf day Ceiling Cat taek naps cuz he werk a lot an dunt even get ovahtiem! **3** Ceiling Cat bless teh sevunf day an he call it Caturday, cuz dat is wen he awl dun wif his werk. An he maek teh Caturday holee.

Adam An Eve

Genesis 2

15 An Ceiling Cat tuk teh man, an put him teh Gardun ov Eden to takez cares ov it cuz Ceiling Cat want anotha day off. **16** An Ceiling Cat sez to teh man, "Yu can has noms on evereeting: **17** but yu see dat tree ovah der? Dat teh Tree of Knowledge, yu no eets dat or yu can has teh deth."

18 An Ceiling Cat sez, "Teh man is awl aloen an dat iz bad. He need sum frendz so Iz gunna maek him a gud frend. (Iz gud at

Oh hai, yu can has frend. She liek yu but missin somefings.

dis stuff, srsly. An it will kepe him outta trubbel.)"

19 An owt ov teh floor Ceiling Cat maed awl teh aminals owtsied an in teh baf tub, an awl teh burdies up in teh sky (an sum liek ostrichusus who no fly, jus fer fun). He browt dem to teh man to see wat he wud call dem. Wutevah teh man cawled dem, teh aminal wuz stuck wif dat naem, an if dey no liek it, tuf tamahlayz!

20 An teh man naem awl ov teh aminals; teh burdiez, teh moo-cow liek aminals, an even teh monstahs ov teh baf tub. But Ceiling Cat wuz sad cuz teh man haf no frendz, an aminals can no chat in chatroom. **21** An Ceiling Cat maek teh man fawl aslepe, an tuk him to teh vet. He taek wun of teh man's ribs cuz it has a flavr. **22** An Ceiling Cat maed teh man a frend frum teh rib an show it to her, and sez, "Oh hai, yu can has frend. She liek yu but missin somefings." **23** Teh man sez,

"Dese bonez iz mai bonez an dis meatz are mai meatz; I cawl her "whoa man", k cuz she iz in ur chest, takin ur ribs. Srsly"

24 So man muv owt ov teh baesment an lievs wif da whoaman, an sez, "Yu can put yer toofbrush necks to mien an iz no eats yu."

An teh man sez, "ORLY?"
Teh whoaman sez, "YA RLY!"
An teh man sez, "No wai!"
An teh whoaman sez, "Wai!"
25 An teh man an whoaman whar INVISIBLE CLOTHES!

Oh Noes, Teh Fall

Genesis 3

1 Nao teh snakez wuz moar sneekay den any beest ov teh feeld wich Ceiling Cat maed. An he mewed to teh whoaman "Yu no can has froot frum teh gardun? Nawt evun teh froot on teh plaets?"

2 An teh whoaman laffed, "Iz can has awl teh froot Iz want, srsly. Whar yu get yer nuez. **3** Teh only frootz Iz no can eetz is teh froot frum teh speshul tree in teh middul of teh gardun. Ceiling Cat sez Iz get ded if Iz eets dat."

4 An teh snaek wuz liek, "Wut? Yu no get ded! **5** Ceiling Cat kno dat, he not tellin yu evereefing. If yu eetz frum dat froot yu can has vishun liek Ceiling Cat. Srsly."

6 Teh whoaman luk at teh tree an she fink it be a gud froot wif a flavr. An she wuz finkin it maek her awl wies an stuff liek Ceiling Cat. So she nom nom nom teh froot an den gif sum to teh man. An teh man nom nom nom tu. **7**

An den dey relized dat dey had no furs liek teh otha aminals an dey saw dat invisible clothes wer invisible an dey sew togedder fig leefs tu hied teh nawty pawts. An Eve maed teh furst thong but it wuz reely itchee.

8 Oh noes! Dey heer Ceiling Cat meowing fer dem in teh gardun an dey got awl scaredy an hied in teh leefs of teh booshes. Dey jus invehnt teh gaem ov hied an seek but dis wuz nawt so fun akshually. **9** An Ceiling Cat cawl owt an sez, "Wut yu nom nom? Wuz it gud?"

10 An Adam wuz liek, "I heer yu commin an Iz gotz awl scaredy. So I hied. I was jus nom nomin an stuffs, srsly! I kind ov akshually nom teh rly rly gud frootz."

11 An Ceiling Cat go, "Did yu eet teh froot of teh Tree of Knowledge? Who told yu to eet dat froot dat Iz say to no eet?"

12 An Adam sez bak, "Teh whoaman told me to eets it! She sez, 'Oh hai. Eet dis. Rly gud.'

So she

nom nom nom teh froot

an den gif sum to teh man.

Stephie.Val

At furst I was liek, 'DO NOT WANT!' but den Iz gotz hungree an Iz nom nom nom teh froots."

13 An Ceiling Cat luk at teh whoaman an sez, "Wut did yu dun? Wut happun?" An the whoman sez, "Oh...hai... teh snaek trikkid me! Dat snaek is wun smartee pantz."

14 An Ceiling Cat sez to teh snaek, "Yu in big trubbel. Cuz yu so bad,

Iz gunna curse yu worser den teh moo-cows,

Akshually, yu gunna get it wurser den teh four legged aminals dat were maed,

Yu gunna slied on yer belly to getz arownd, srsly. I taek yer legs!

An gif dem to teh French an dey gunna eetz it an cawl it "frog legz"

An on top ov awl dat, yu gunna eetz teh dust.

Frum yer burf to teh day yu die.

An wurse ov awl, yu gets no cookiez. Yu awlso get no cheezeburger. NO CAN HAS. Srsly.

15 An iz gunna maek teh bad stuffz,

Between yu an teh whoaman

An between her babehz an yer babez,

He gunna maek owies on yer head,

An yu gunna maek owies on his heel, srsly.

16 To teh whoaman he wus liek,

"Wen yu gif babehz tis gunna hurt lotz;

It gunna hurtz so much yu yell at yer husban.

An he iz nawt gunna liek dat

An he gunna pwn yu an ask fer beers an sammiches."

17 An to Ceiling Cat wuz mad at Adam tu. An he sez to Adam,

"Teh urf, I curs its

An yu gunna werk yer butt off awl teh tiem

An itz gunna be hard to maek teh cheezburgers.

Srsly.

18 Teh urf gunna gif yu thornies and othah sharp stuffz

An yu gunna eets teh plantz dat yu werk reel hard fer.

19 An yu gunna getz reel hot werkin

Yu gunna eet onlee teh fud yu maek,

Until yu kik teh bukkit an getz bureed liek yer poop in the littuhbocks,

Yu wer maed frum dust

An yu ar dust,

An wen yu maek ded yu gunna be dust again."

20 An teh man call his wief Eve nao, cuz she wuz teh mother of awl teh livin things, srsly. An awlso cuz Bertha wuz nawt a gud naem, srsly.

Noah's Reely Big Bowt

Genesis 6

An Ceiling Cat saw dat awl ov teh kittehs ov teh Urf wer wikkid an stuff. An dey rip up awl ov teh toylet papur an trie an pretend dey no do it. An dey riet wikkid-pedia to teech awl teh othur kitteh hao to be bad kittehs.

6 An Ceiling Cat wuz rly rly sad he maed to kittehs and teh Urf. He wuz awlso veri mad at dem fer bein so bad!

7 An Ceiling Cat sez, "Iz gunna pwn teh Urfz. Cuz dey so bad. Iz gunna pwn teh moo-cows, teh creepie tings, teh burdz, an

Maek gynormus boat cawled a Ark ov gophr wud an maek rumz in teh ark

Fer forti days teh watter coem down frum teh Ceiling, an teh watter roes an roes an roes on teh Urf

awl of teh lief. Iz so sry I maed dem, srsly."

8 But Ceiling Cat thawt Noah wuz wun kewl cat, rly.

9 Dis is teh storee ov Noah. Noah wuz wun ritechus dood, an liek mor ritechus den aniwun else. Noah hung out wif Ceiling Cat alot an lissend tu tunez an played Pokemons an stuff. An sumtiem Ceiling Cat even letz him winz cuz he lieked him alot.

13 An Ceiling Cat sez tu Noah, "Iz gunna pwn teh whoel Urf cuz teh Urf has moar evilz an bad stuffz den WoW an GTA putz togedder. So iz gunna pwnz dem an teh whoel Urf. Awl teh filez in kittehs heds ish awl messed up wif virusez an dey keep emailin em tu awl der frendz. Iz shud haev kept it in Beta longah an maeded anti-viruz an stuff to keep owt teh viruses an rootkitz an stuf liek dat. Srsly.

14 Maek gynormus boat cawled a Ark ov gophr wud an maek rumz in teh ark, an cover it wif tar on teh insiedz an outsiedz.

Genesis 7

Ceiling Cat den sez, **2** "Noah, Goes into teh ark, yu an yer kittenz, cuz yu kewl an ritechus an stuff in dis generashun. Taek wif yu sevun ov evri kind ov clean moo-cow, male an wief, an two ov evri kind of unclean moo-cow, male an its wief. **3** An awlso sevun ov evri kind ov burd, male an femael cuz teh burdz are scaredz of teh comitmunts, an awlso sevun ov evri kind ov burd, male an female (fer teh saem reesun) tu keep der kindz livin thruowt teh urfs, fer sevun daiz frum nao Iz gunna send teh wetness on teh Urf. A littul advise, it probubly a gud idea to keep 'em seperit so teh moo-cows don't haev an episoed ov secksy tiem until joo get der. **4** Fer fowty daiz and fowty nites, it gunna be wet and Iz gunna pwn some n00bs."

5 An Noah did wut Ceiling Cat told him to, an put in teh drie wall betwen teh moo-cows an his sons and his dotters so dey wud nawt do nething liek to maek cowz go want secksy tiem during teh fowty daiz.

6 Noah was liek rly old wen teh wetness come. **7** An Noah and his kittehs enter teh Ark so dey wudnt get teh wetness in der furz. **8** Awl teh moo-cows an teh otha stuff. **9** Male an femael, caem to Noah an he dun put dem in teh Ark, as Ceiling Cat command him. **10** An aftah teh sevun daiz teh wetness caem.

11 In da liek sicks-hundred yeerz ov Noah's lief, on teh sevunteenth dai ov teh secund monf Ceiling Cat lef teh baftub spowt runnin an it overflo frum teh ceiling. **12** An teh wetness caem to teh Urf an it wus awl wet. Srsly.

13 On dat der dai, teh sons of Noahz, Shem, Japheth, and Ham (nawt teh meet, lol) tuk wif dem der wivez, **14** an dey tuk evri kind ov aminal dat Ceiling Cat maed accordin to it kind, **15** two ov dem, srsly. **16** An teh aminals wer male and femael jus liek Ceiling Cat sez. An Ceiling Cat told Noah to leef teh dragonz an unicornz behindz, cuz he no liek dem much. So Ceiling Cat sez to dose aminals, "OK. Yu stai heer, iz be rite bak."

17 Fer forti days teh watter coem down frum teh Ceiling, **18** an teh watter roes an roes an roes on teh Urf, an teh ark float on teh watter. **19** Teh watter wuz so high it cover teh big mowntins dat wer high liek teh big bukshelf. **20** Teh watter roes rly high, liek moar den twenty feet abov teh mowntins, OMGWTFBBQ!! **21** Evri aminal be ded on teh Urf. Awl teh moo-cows, teh burdies, an slipperi creechurs no has lief no moar. **22** Awl teh aminals dat breef thru der nowstuls be ded. **23** Onlee teh aminals dat go on teh Ark wif Noah wer no ded.

24 Teh watter flood teh Urf fer liek wun-hundrid-fifti dais, srsly.

Genesis 8

13 An so Noah wuz gettin boered an stuffz an he gettin tired ov cleenin aftah teh moo-cows, so he peek owt. **14** An by teh twenti-sevenf dai teh big sandbocks wus awlmost redy to use. Srsly!

15 An Ceiling Cat sez to Noah, **16** "GTFO, yu an yer wiefs an yer boy-kittehs an der wiefs. **17** An taek owt awl ov teh aminals frum teh Ark an let dem haf lotz of secksy tiem awl ovah to maek teh Urf filled wif dem!"

18 So Noah caem owt wif his boy-kittehs an wiefs an awl dey wiefs. **19** An Awl teh aminals in teh Ark awlso caem owt, liek, in ordur an stuffz.

Oh hai, letz maek reel tall towerz for us so we be togethr fer-evar!

Teh Towur ov Babel

Genesis 11

1 An awl teh kittehs be speekin teh saem lolspeak, srsly. **2** Whiel teh kittehs be moovin east, dey finded vallee in teh land uv Shinar an sit der. **3** Dey sez "Oh hai, letz maek teh brix an make em hard wif fier. Plus fier gud fer sleepin by. Srsly." So dey use teh brix fer stone an bitumen (Wut dat?) fer mortar. **4** Den dey sez "Oh hai, letz maek reel tall towerz for us so we be togethr fer-evar!"

5 So, Ceiling Cat comeded down an saw teh kittehs an der towerz. **6** Den Ceiling Cat sez "Oh noes, if dey awl togethr aftah mah high spot, dey gonna get mah high spot! **7** Iz gots to confuzzle dem an stop dem!" **8** Dat's wai Ceiling Cat pwned dem an drag dem awai frum der towerz. Dey stop buldin aftah dat. **9** So teh towerz wuz naemed Babel cuz Ceiling Cat made teh men babbul der befer moovin dem.

Joseph

Genesis 37

This iz story ov Jacob. Dis reely story of Joseph but teh kittehs who rited teh Bible rited it down rong. Joseph wus 17 yeer old kitteh an wun dai he an his bros wus givin cookies tu teh sheeplez. An Joseph wuz a tattel-kitteh an told hiz old man awl teh wikkid stuffs dey did like raedin wikkid-pedia an masturbatin an smokin weedz an stealin kittehs stuffs an stuff.

3 Nao Israel, who reel naem wus Jacob, lieked Joseph moar den awl his othr kittens, cuz he wus old kitteh wehn Joseph wuz bornd. So he wuz liek grandsun wich iz moar fun: an he maed him sum badass pimp cloths an some totally 1337 kickz an wud ov gaev him a totally trickd out ride but cars wusnt thawt ov yet. **4** An when his bros saw dat Jacob lieked Joseph moar den dem, dey haetz him an getz awl angree an stuf.

An dey getz all up in hiz face an sed reely rood meen fings tu him.

5 An Joseph can has weerd dreem, an he told his bros wich wuz reely stoopid n00b thing to do: An dey haetz him alot moar an getz even mor angree an stuf. **6** An he sez to dem, "Lissen up d00dz, I can has wieerd dreem liek dis: **7** We wuz in ur feeld harvestin ur weetz, cuz it wuz farmerz dai off (cuz dey maed Untied Farmwerkerz Unyon, dammit), an awl yer weetz wuz bowin to my weetz."

8 An his bros sez tu him, "WTF yu ben smokin? Yu think yu be king or sumthin? Yu thinkz yu is teh bosscat ov us?" An dey haatz him evun moar cuz ov his dreems An wat he sed to dem.

12 An his bros go to Shechem to getz moar cookiez fer teh sheepz. **13** An Israel whos reel naem wuz Jacob sez to Joseph, "Did yer bros go to Shechem to getz cookiez fer teh sheepz? Iz

wantz yu to goez an maek shur dey alrite." An Joseph sed "K."

14 An he sed to him, "Go find owt if yer bros an teh sheepz iz alrite. An coem bak an tellz me." So Joseph sed "K, goen to Shechem, BRB." **15** An he gotz losted (teh internetz map wus nawt to gret ackshually) an sum dood finded him an ask him, "Wut yu lookin fer?"

16 An he sed, "Iz lookin fer my bros who iz goen to getz cookiez fer teh sheepz."

17 An teh dood sed, "Dey ar goen an dey sed, 'Letz goez to Dothan cuz dey has bettur cookiez der.'" An Joseph sed, "Kthxbai," an finded his bros in Dothan. **18** An wen dey seez him an he wuz still on teh roadz long wais awai lookin fer dem, dey decied to pwnz him.

19 An dey sed, "Look doods, teh kid dat haz teh weerd dreemz is comin. **20** So letz pwn him, An thro him into sum pit, an we gunna say sum evil aminal like crocodiel or lion or lolrus

eeted him: An to hell wif hiz dreems, LOL."

21 An Reuben heardz dem, an he sed, "Dont pwnz him cuz yu will lose pointz. **22** So dont pwnz him, jus thro him in sum pit way owt in teh booniez, an dont hurtz him." Reuben kind of liek Joseph an wuz sort ov suk up too an thot he miet taekz him bak to his old man wen nowun wuz lookin, but he no tellz dem dat.

23 An so wen Joseph finded his bros, dey took awai his totally badass closths, an his totally 1337 kickz too. but dey cud no taek hiz pimp ried cuz cars no thawt ov yet. **24** An they thro him into teh pit an der wuz no watters in it. no cheezburgerz or cookiez eether.

25 An it wuz tiem fer lunch so dey sitz down an eetz cheezburgerz an cookiez. An dey sawed a crew ov Ishmealites frum Gilead goin to Egypt wif lotz ov camels an all kindz ov reely gud herbz an weetz an othur reely gud stufz liek catnipz.

26 An Judah sed, "I can has good idea! We no pwnz him, we sellz him and has a money. **27** We no has to pwnz him if we can sellz him." An his bros sed "K."

28 Den dey met sum Midianites; an dey taek Joseph owt ov teh pit, an sellz him to dem fer 20 moniez: an dey taek Joseph to Egypt. **29** An laeter Reuben caem bak to teh pit; An seez dat Joseph wuz goen. An he toer up his cloths cuz dats wot peepul did wen dey wuz liek all sad an emo an stuff bak in teh dai. **30** An he sez to his bros, "Joeseph iz awl goen, WTF ar we gunna do nao?"

31 An dey tuk Joseph's totaly badass cloths, an killz wun ov teh goats an puts teh blood awl ovah teh cloths an letz teh othuh goatz eet teh totaly 1337 kickz.

32 An they browt teh cloths to der owld man an sed, "We founded dese totaly badass cloths. Ar dey Joseph's cloths or not."

33 An he knew it, an sed, "Dese mah son's cloths! Sum evul aminal eeted him liek he wuz cookie. Joseph is fer shur torn up in litel peeces. Srsly."

34 An Jacob toer up his cloths, an put on sackcloth dat wuz reely scratchi, an wuz all sad an emo fer reely long tiem. **35** An awl his wiefs an kittenz trys to maek him feelz moer bettur but wuz no workin. An he sed, "Iz gonna be awl sad an emo til Iz ded." So he kept on bein awl sad an emo an stuff.

Moses an teh Scari Burnin Bush

Exodus 2

1 Sum guy go to Levi's plaes an marryed hiz dotter. **2** An teh dotter had a kitten hoo wuz a boy-kitteh so she hied him. **3** So she do wot Pharo sed an put him in teh rivur, but she maed a bukkit fer him so he no be ded in teh watter. An she sed, "Pharo is liek reely laem fer tellin us puts kittehs in teh rivur an not sai yu no can has bukkitz! LOL stoopid Pharo!" **4** An his big sis Miriam wuz der too an she hied an wotch him floet awai an she like, "Kthxbai." An teh crocodielz an teh lolrusz did not eeted him, wich wuz gud cuz if dey did der wudnt be no moar storyz an dis wud be reely short buk.

5 An teh Princess wus nekkid in ur riiver havin baffs cuz she reely liek baffs. An she sawed teh widdle kitten an got him owt. **6** An teh baby crie, an teh princess wuz liek "Whoa! A Hebruw! An he iz teh kyoot. DO WANT!"

7 An Miriam wuz teh reely smart kid an she sed "Shud I get a Hebruw-kitteh to taek caer ov it?"

8 An teh Princess wuz liek, "Yea." So Miriam go bak to her momcats base an sed, "Whoa mom, teh princess find mah kid bro an she want Hebruw momcat to taeks caer ov him an yu can go to teh princess base an do dat. Hao kewl iz dat?" **9** Princess wuz Pharo's dotter, BTW, srsly. An she sed to teh Hebruw ladee hoo wuz reely teh kitten's momcat, "Yu can has a money fer bein kitten-sittur." An she sed, "K." Cuz Hebruw kitteh wuz thinkin, "Whoa dis mah babee." She no say dis owt lowd. **10** An wen he wuz groen up, teh Princess sed, "Ur naem is Moses, srsly. Cuz dat meenz Iz tuk yu owt ov teh riverz an stuf."

OMG dis bush, dis bush, dis bush iz on fire! An is still on teh fires!

11 Moses awl big kitteh nao! Wun day he go see his frenz. Dey is werkin hard. Den Moses see sum Egyptian d00d beetin up a Jew-kitteh liek him. **12** So Moses luk rownd an maek suer no otha kitteh rownd, an he maek teh bad kitteh ded! Moses hied to bodee an maek invisible bodee. **13** An den Moses saw two Jew-kittehs fitin! An Moses wuz liek, "Why yu fitin eachodder! Yu can has frenzship!" **14** An teh guy wus liek, "Yu nawt teh bos of meh. Yu gunna maek me ded liek dat Egyptian-kitteh? Hah!" Moses wus scaredy cat nao, hao did teh guy kno?

15 An teh Pharo herd bout awl dis an wus liek, "WUT! DO NOT WANT!" an Moses hied cuz he kno want to be ded.

Exodus 3

1 Moses taek teh sheepz to teh Ceiling Cat mownten. **2** I'm in ur bush, burnin, not consumin. **3** Moses sez "OMG dis bush, dis bush, dis bush iz on fire! An is still on teh fires!"

4 An Ceiling Cat sez "Moses Moses! Yo over teh heer!" An Moses be liek, "Wut?"

5 An Ceiling Cat sez "Taek off yer shoos, dis be teh holiez plase. **6** Iz be teh Ceiling Cat. Awl ur dadz are belong to me." An Moses wuz scared.

7 Ceiling Cat sez, "All teh peepul be sad. I see dat. **8** Iz comin to saev dem an bring dem lotz ov cheezburgers an milks. An honeys. **9** Iz heerz teh peepuls cryin an stuf an teh bad guys wif teh pyramids iz bad guys. **10** So, Iz sending yu to teh peepul to saev dem, k?"

11 An Moses wuz all liek, "Wuh? Me? Nowai!" **12** An Ceiling Cat wuz liek, "Wai. Iz helpin yu, an yu bring teh peepuls to wership teh Ceiling Cat at Ceiling Cat Mownten."

13 An Moses wuz liek, "Wut if teh peeps say, 'Who iz dat guy der?'"

14 An Ceiling Cat wuz liek, "I yam who I yam.

15 Ferevrs, dat be meh."

Teh Ten Bad Plagues

Exodus 6

28 Itz so nise, da Bible say it twise: Ceiling Cat sez to Moses, **29** "Tawk wif Pharo teh stuf Iz tellin yu."

30 Moses sez, "I no can! I just m-m-m-meow liek dis. Pharo no lissen to meh. He just covur eers and sing 'Lalalala! Iz no heer yu!'"

Exodus 7

1 Dn Ceiling Cat sez to Moses, "Yu iz like Ceiling Cat to Pharo, an Aaron iz yer prophit. **2** Yu sez what I tells yu, an Aaron do stufs too. Wen Aaron tells Pharo to let yer doodz go **3** I maek Pharo awl meen an say no, **4** an den Iz be in Pharo's Egypt judgin his Egypt doodz. **5** An Pharo will kno Iz gotz ninja powerz den."

6 Moses an Aaron did wat dey wuz told. **7** Moses wuz 80 An Aaron was 83 wen dey tawk to Pharo.

8 Ceiling Cat sez to Moses an Aaron, **9** "Wen Pharo sez 'Do kewl stufs wif powerz,' frow yer stik onna grownd, An it will be a snaek."

10 So Moses an Aaron went to seez teh Pharo. Aaron frew his stick onna grownd, an WTF its a snaek! **11** Pharo got sum magik-kittehs to do fancy stufs. **12** Pharo's magik-kittehs awlso maed sum snaekz, but Aaron's snaek eeted dem. **13** But Pharo sez, "So whut?"

Teh Plague ov Blud

Exodus 7

14 Den Ceiling Cat sez, "Pharo is no fun, an is keepin ur doodz. **15** Go see Pharo tomarow wen he iz on da Nile. Don' ferget yer stick. **16** Den yu say, 'Let mah doodz go!' **17** An den yu put ur stick inna water, and OMGWTF it be blud an stinky, **18** an Egypt doodz no can has fish an no can has drinkz an no can has baffs eether."

20 So Moses an Aaron did wat dey wuz towld. **21** An BLARG teh fish ar ded. An teh kittehs wuz awl sad cuz no can has fish an has to eetz meeses evri day an dey sed, "BOOOOOORRRRRRING!!!!!!"

Teh Plague ov teh Frogz

Exodus 8

1 Ceiling Cat sez to Moses, "Tell Pharo 'Ceiling Cat sez let mah doodz go, so dey can wership me. **2** If yu sez no, I maek frogeez awl ovur yer whole country. **3** Teh Nile can has frogz. Frogz will be in ur base, an in ur bed, an in ur doodz howses, an in ur kitchens. **4** Teh frogz will be awl on ur peepuls. An dey will be in ur bukkitz makin der tadpoels. An der wont be anee French doodz to eetz dm cuz French doods wuznt invented yet. So der.'"

6 So Aaron held his stik owt ovur teh watter, an frogz wus awl ovur Pharo's base, jumpin on his doodz.

12 Aftur Moses an Aaron left Pharo's base, Moses yeld to Ceiling Cat abowt teh frogz. **13** And Ceiling Cat herd him, an BLARG teh frogz ar ded. **14** Big piles ov ded frogz wer maed, an it wuz stinky. **15** But wen Pharaoh saw teh frogpilez, his heart wuz hard, an he wuz like "I no can heer Moses an Aaron."

The Plague ov teh Gnats

Genesis 8

16 So Ceiling Cat sez to Moses, "Tell Aaron to hit teh grownd wif his stik, an awl ovur Egypt teh dust will tern into gnats." 17 Dey did, an gnats wus awl in Pharo's Egypt. 18 An dis tiem, teh magik-kittehs cud no maek gnats.

19 Teh magik-kittehs sed to Pharo, "I fink Ceiling Cat is fo reel." But Pharo's hart wuz still hard.

Teh Plague ov teh Fliez

Exodus 8

20 So Ceiling Cat sez to Moses, "Waek up reely an say to Pharo, 'Ceiling Cat sez, 'Let mah doodz go.' **21** If yu do nawt, Iz send flies on yu and ur doodz an ur peepulz.'"

22 But Iz leeve Goshen alone, cuz is teh Israelites base. An yu will kno dat I, Ceiling Cat, am in Goshen protectin mah doodz. **23** Iz maek mah doodz an ur doodz differunt. Yu sees it tomarow!"

24 And Ceiling Cat sho it teh necks day. Bunches of flies

Bunches of flies flewed into Pharo's base an into his doodz howses.

flewed into Pharo's base an into his doodz howses. An sum ov teh Egyptians sed, 'Wish der wuz stil sum frogz to eetz awl dees flies,' but sum othur Egyptians sed, 'STFU,' so dey sed, 'K,' an shutted up.

25 Den Pharo asks Moses an Aaron, "Kill stufs for Ceiling Cat heer in Egypt."

26 But Moses sez, "Do not want. Egypt doodz wud be grossed owt, an hit us wif roks. **27** We hazta go awai fer three dayz to gif Ceiling Cat ded stufs. Is orders."

28 Pharo sez, "OK, but yu bettur nawt go far. Nao, yu prey fer meh."

29 Moses sez, "I pray aftur Iz go. Tomarow teh fliez wil leev ur base. But no moar triks, Pharo - yu hasta let mah doodz go offer sacurfices."

30 Den Moses pray to Ceiling Cat. **31** An Ceiling Cat wus kewl an maed awl teh fliez go home. **32** But dis tiem Pharo maeks his hart hard an wud not let teh Israelite doodz go.

Teh Plague ov teh Ded Moocows

Exodus 9

1 Den Ceiling Cat sed to Moses, "Go sey to Pharo, 'Dis is wut say Ceiling Cat, 'Teh Ceiling Cat ov teh Hebruws, let meh doodz go, will ya?' **2** Srsly, **3** If yu no do, Ceiling Cat will maek ded awl ur aminals! He will! Awl teh horsies, teh dawnkees, teh humpty kamels, teh baa-sheeps, teh moo-cows an teh goatz. **4** But Ceiling Cat wont maek hiz kittehs aminals cos dat be meen!"

5 So Ceiling Cat set a tiem, "Tomarow at fiev-ish!" **6** So teh necks day Ceiling Cat did it an all teh animals ov teh Egyptians gots run ovur by Ceiling Cat but nawt his kitteh's aminals. **7** Pharo was like "WOAH!" He sent owt boorucats to chek an dey sawed dat Israel aminals wer okey-dokey, but he stil no let Ceiling Cat's kittehs go.

Teh Plague ov Owchie-Blisturs

Exodus 9

8 An Ceiling Cat got Moses an Aaron to chuk soot at Pharo. **9** It spred an maed awl teh kittehs get owchie-blisturs.

10 An so dey thro it an evriwun gets liek awl owchie-blisturs ova dem. **11** An magishuns try to magik teh owchie-blisturs awai but no werk **12** But Pharo wus like "Watevur!" an stil nevur let teh kittehs go.

Teh Plague ov teh Big Ice

Exodus 9

13 Ceiling Cat say to Moses "Tell Pharo dat he bettur let dem doodz go, **14** or dis tiem iz gonna send big ice on everiwun even teh servents an even peepul ovur in China an Canada an ever wher an teh hole Urf so dat yu kno Iz a big deel **15** I coulda hert ya befor **16** but Iz want yu peepul to kno mah naem. **17** Yu ar gunna pay fer dis Pharo! **18** Dis tiem tomarow its gunna be such bad ice **19** Yu hied yur aminals or dey gunna be struk by teh big ice.

20 Pharo puts awl teh aminals in his howse **21** But whoeva no lissen to Ceiling Cat left der slaves an aminals in teh feelds.

22 Ceiling Cat told Moses to put his paws up. **23** An den Moses put his paws up **24** An big ice caem down. **25** Teh big ice smush a few peepul an aminals, **26** but Ceiling Cat maed Israel safe.

27 Teh Pharo got Moses an sed, "OK, I has doen a big invisabul error, Ceiling Cat is rite. **28** Pleed wif teh Ceiling Cat, Iz gunna let everiwun go nao."

29 Moses sez, "Soon as Iz can leeve dis city der be no more thundur an big ice, k? **30** Yu need be scardy to Ceiling Cat! Kthnx."

31 Nao teh barley be ded, no gunna maek beer **32** Wheatz ar gud.

33 Moses left teh city an teh big ice stop. **34** Wen Pharo sawed it stop he made anothur invisabul error. **35** So he sed, "Wait a min, yur doodz no goin nowhere!"

Teh Plague ov teh Flyin Buggies

Exodus 10

3 So Moses an Aaron went to Pharo an sed to him, "Ceiling Cat sez, Supreme Kitteh ov teh Hebrews, 'Hao long do Iz hafta wait til yu let mah doosz owt? **4** Iz gunna open dis box ov flyin buggies. **5** An der wil be so many dat yu wont be able to see trees no moar. **6** An dey goin into awl teh howses an mess eveyfing up!'" So Moses an Aaron left.

7 An Pharo frenz gots mad an sed "Hao long yu gunna be lettin teh doodz go? Hurry cuz Iz dunt want no buggies on me!"

12 An teh Ceiling Cat sed to Moses "Strech ur paws owt."

13 Den it got reely windy an sum locusts caem an blew everywhar **14** An teh locusts went everywhar all ovur. **15** Dey covered teh faces in teh hole Urf an dey eets awl teh froots.

16 Teh Pharaoh meow fer Moses an Aaron an he sed "Iz dun anothur invisable error! **17** Nao yu can go an da kittehs."

18 An he went to Pharo an called Ceiling Cat. **19** An teh Ceiling Cat got awl teh locusts to go bai bai. **20** But den Pharo change his mind

Teh Plague ov teh Dark

Exodus 10

21 An da Ceiling Cat sed to Moses "Luk, Iz gunna turn teh lites off so it be reely dark, kay? So dark dat kittehs no see." **22** An Moses strech his arms out an den it wus dark **23** But he let kittehs in Israel-part has lit.

24 An Pharo change bak his mind an sed dat teh kittehs cud go.

25 An Moses sed "OK. **26** But weer bringin teh moo-cows wiv us."

27 But den Pharo change his mind! **28** Den Pharo sed "Stai away frum me Moses! Kthxbai."

29 An Moses sed "Fien Den!"

Luk, Iz gunna turn teh lites off so it be reely dark, kay? So dark dat kittehs no see.

I'M DEAD
Den, awl oldest kittens in Egypt ar maed ded. Fall down, go boom!

Teh Plague ov teh Ded Furstborn

Exodus 11

1 Ceiling Cat dez to Moses, "Wun mor plaig. Dis tiem fer shur. Dis tiem yu can has exit visa frum Egypt. **2** Tellz ur male kittehs an female kiteahs to ask fer silber an goald frum der Egyptian neybor doodz. **3** Dey be OK wif givven yu dat stuf. Dey likes yu guyz. I fixxed it dat wey, k?"

4 Moses sez to Pharaoh, "Midnites, I can has niec stroll arownd Egypt. Not so niec reezun why I can has niec stroll." **5** Den, awl oldest kittens in Egypt ar maed ded. Fall down, go boom! Pharo numbur wun kitten be maed ded too. Slaev numbur wun kitten ded too. Evun moo-cow's numbur wun moo-cow babeh be

ded. **6** All Egypt cry an cry. **7** But no cryin in teh Israel howsez. Even dogz no bark neer Israel howzes. Ceiling Cat fixs things gud. **8** Den yu will giv us teh royal boot, an we be owt of Egypt. Yay! kthxbai!" Den angri Moses stomp awai frum Pharo.

9 Ceiling Cat sed to Moses, "Pharo no lissen, so yu gotta go wif teh stroll, an Iz taek teh toll." **10** Ceiling Cat wuz rite! Pharo no lissen. He no let teh Israelites owt. Boo to Pharo fer hiz Invisibul Error!

Exodus 12

29 Itz Midniet an all hell braik loos! All teh numur wun kittens ov Egypt go "Blargh Iz ded." **30** All uv Egypt cry an cry.

"Leev Egypt, Nao!"

Exodus 12

31 Dat nite, Pharo sez to Moses an Aaron, "Awl Israel GTFO uv Egypt nao. Srsly. **32** Taik ur aminals too an ur flox. An say hai to Ceiling Cat fer meh, k?"

33 Egyptians say to Isaelites "OMFG! Go befoer we awl goz 'Blargh!'". **34** So Israelites grab der bred an carri it wif dem. **35** An Israel kittehs ask Egyptians "BTW, we can has yer bling?" **36** Dey get goald an silber bling frum Egyptians. Ceiling Cat fix it gud.

Exodus 13

17 So wen teh Pharo letz teh Israel-kittehs go, Ceiling Cat said don go to Philistine land, tho dat closur cuz Ceiling Cat sed, "Dem kittehs miet poop der pantz if dey sees war an go back to Egypt." **18** So Ceiling Cat took kittehs on scenic root thru Sea of Reeds. Teh Israelites wuz runnun out of Egypt.

20 Dey leev Succoth (Booths), an camped owt at Etham, neer te big wildernez. **21** Ceiling Cat went in front uf dem in a clowd in teh day, so dey don get lost, an as pillar uf fier at nite so dey can seez whar dey goin, so dey cud travel awl day an nite. **22** Teh cloud an teh fier no ditch dem to cach a movie.

Crossin teh Reed Sea

Exodus 14

5 So Pharo wus liek, "OMG whar did dey go?!" Cuz dey awl left alreddy. An he an his kittehs change der minds abowt lettin dem go. Teh Egyptians wer sad cuz der slaves awl left. **6** An den Pharo got in hiz Pharo-cheryit an wus liek, "C'mon guyz lets get teh slaves bak!" **7** Pharo went aftur teh Israelites wif leik 600 ov hiz bestest armi d00ds. Srsly. **8** So stubburn Pharo chayse dem an Israel wus all, "Bai, sry." **9** But Pharo an his cheryits chayse dem moar an he cach up wif teh Isrealites at teh Reed Sea. **10** Den teh Israelites saw Egyptians an wer awl, "OMFG!" **11** So teh Isrealites wer reel mad at Moses cuz dey no want to be ded! Dey awl "Why we hafta maek ded heer? We wud be ded in Egypt anywai." **12** Dey wud rathur do evryfing fer teh Egyptians den be ded.

13 So Moses sed, "OMG, chillowt, srsly! Ceiling Cat sez wer totawly gud. Yu no see Egyptians animoar. **14** Ceiling Cat will gif yu cheezburgers! I promis yu all! Dun moov!" **15** So Ceiling Cat sez "Whai yu awl scaredy an askin fer halp? Keep moovin. **16** Holdz up ur big stik ovur teh sea. Teh sea will splitz apart, srsly! An yu an teh Israelites can walk on grownd an not get wet becuz DO NOT WANT! **17** An cuz teh Egyptians, dey stubburn, dey chayse yu. but Iz wil pwnz dem all. **18** An aftur pwnzing, teh Egyptians kno I is teh Ceiling Cat." **19** So teh big clowd dat wuz Ceiling Cat wuz in frunt but it mooved to teh bak. **20** So it wer between teh Egyptians an teh Israelites. An teh clowd wuz dark scarey clowd fur teh Egyptians, but wuz niec happeh clowd fur teh Israel doods. An teh armies no can see cuz it wer dark. **21** Moses put his paw ovur teh sea, an Ceiling Cat mayk big wind dat blowd teh sea awl nite till der wuz dry land so kittehs no get wet. Teh waterz wer divided. **22** Teh Israelites cross teh sea on dry grownd an no get wet, but der wuz walls ov watter on teh sied. **23** But teh Egyptians an teh charyots chaysed dem. **24** Den, rite befur sun caem up, Ceiling Cat looked at teh Egyptians an he pwnz dem so dey freek owt. **25** An teh weelz ov teh cheryits wuz stuk an not moov gud. Teh Egyptians sed, "Ceiling Cat fites fer justis fer teh Israelites, an he no liek us. We shud go awai, liek srsly." **26** Ceiling Cat sed to Moses, "Hold ur paw ovur teh sea, an teh watters, dey coem bak an covur teh Egyptians." **27** So moses hold his paw ovur teh sea, an teh watters go bak to normul. Teh Egyptians try to run awai, but Ceiling Cat frew dem into teh sea. **28** Teh watters cover teh cheryits an awl teh Egyptian army doodz. Nawt wun Egyptian dood cud get awai frum teh watters. **29** But teh Israelites, dey cross teh sea on dry grownd an no get wet. **30** So Ceiling Cat saev teh Israel kittehs dat day. An teh Isrealites see teh Egyptians ded on teh beech. **31** An teh Israelites see dat Ceiling Cat can pwn Egyptians, an dey liek, "Wow dat be awsum!" An dey beleev Ceiling Cat an Moses.

Teh Ten Big Roolz

Exodus 19

1 Aftur awhilz dey fownd dis desert wif some sand an stuff. 2 Dey lay on teh sofas by da big mowntain an snoozed.

3 Ceiling Cat sed, "Oh hai Moses! Tell ur doods 4 remembuh awl teh cheezburgers I gif yu an dat othur stuff too. 5 Oh! An do what Iz say an Iz be protectin yu liek yus mai fambily. 6 Yu guys can be mai posse!"

7 Moses went an told his d00dz 8 an him doodz waz like, "Wai!"

9 Den Ceiling Cat sed, "Iz goin to be in ur magic clowd talkin to ur doodz. 10 So evribuddy go cleans ur litter bockses 11 cause yu got to be reddy wen Iz show up. Iz gunna be on Sinai in mah magik clowd 12 Tell evriwun Iz no want yu on teh mowntain 13 If Iz catch yu on teh mowntain iz gonna eet yu."

14 Moses an his kittehs cleened owt wll der litter bockses, licked demselfs cleen 15 an Moses told him kittehs "Okai. We cleenz nao. No moar gettin derty til afur Ceiling Cat coems bak."

16 Den der wuz big storm and kittehs were like, "OMG-WTFBBQ!" 17 Moses an his kittehs went to see teh Ceiling Cat. 18 Ceiling Cat fell off teh ceiling, and he wuz awl on fier. 19 Moses wus liek, "WTF!" an Ceiling Cat wus liek, "Chill owt d00d."

20 Ceiling Cat told Moses, "Hai! Coem sit neer teh ceiling so Iz can talk to yu bettur." 21 Moses went to talk an Ceiling Cat sed "I like yu okay, but Iz gunna eet ur kittehs if dey get on mah bad sied. 22 Evun teh wuns wif cheezburgers."

23 Moses wus liek "Dey ar under control dood."

24 An Ceiling Cat wus liek, "Okai, okai. Yu can bring Aarron too" 25 An Moses wus liek, "Sweet deal!"

Caturday, yu no werk

Exodus 20

1 Den Ceiling Cat spoked awl dem werds:

2 "Iz Ceiling Cat an Iz Top Cat, an I broughted yu owt of hawt land wif no cheezburgers fer hard werk at awl.

3 No can has other Ceiling Cat! Yu gotz othur Ceiling Cat, I shoot yu wif mah lazer eyes.

4 If yu try be Ceiling Cat of any of mai creashunz up in floaty skai, down in urf or in watter, Iz shoot yu wif mah lazer eyes. 5

If yu think faek Ceiling Cat iz Ceiling Cat, I maek yu ded an ur kittens ded. An if ur kittenz haf kittenz, dey be ded too, for being stupid. **6** f nawt, Iz loev yu an awl ur lotz ov kittens!

7 Yu sez Ceiling Cat bad, Iz shoot yu wif mah lazer eyes, cuz I dun liek it. Srsly.

8 Remembur Caturday an keep holy. **9** Yu werk 6 days an finnish werk, k? **10** Caturday, yu no werk. Yu An awl ur peepz go wership me. An, if yu beez gud, I mek it so yu can stay home an do awl teh stuff yu want to do. **11** I maed ceiling an floor an baftub an awl othur stuff n it - so I maek it holy cuz I no werk.

12 Be gud to papa an mama so yu has long lief.

13 Yu no maek kittehs ded! Srsly!

14 Yu no maek sex wif othur gurlz or menz den ur wief (So no awsum treesum alowed!).

15 Yu no taek stuff fer free if not getz fer free.

16 Yu no tell bad stuff about ur necks dor neibur.

17 Yu no wantz neibur stuff! No wief, no gurlz, no menz, no aminals, an NO BUKKITZ! DEY NOT UR BUKKITZ, K? Dey teh LOLrus' bukkits.

18 Wen kittehs see mai thundur an awl cool speshul effects dey wur scardey wimps

19 Dey sed to Moses, "Yu go speek to uz an we will lissen, but Ceiling Cat will shoot us wif his lazer eyes!"

20 Moses LOL lotz, an a bit moar, for dey wuz such wimps, an sed, "Ceiling Cat no maek yu ded; he just wantz to haf fun wif yu kittehs an maek yu scaredy cats so yu obey him."

21 But teh kittehs wer still wimps an let Moses go der to Ceiling Cat.

David an Goliath teh Giunt

1 Samuel 17

1 Teh Philistine kittes got awl der armies reddy an camp on wun hill. **2** Saul den got awl hiz armies reddy an camp on othur hill. **3** So teh two armies of kittes faec each othur on teh two hillz wft teh vally between dem.

4 Den Goliath, who wuz an awsum champyun caem an looked at teh Israelites. Dis Goliath was ovur nine feet tall. Srsly. **5** He had all kindz of reely sweet armorz an stuff an he wuz jus amazin. **6** An he had a big javelin dat wus sharp an stuf. **7** His speer wuz super hevvy, too. He had anuther kitteh carry hiz stufz fer him.

8 Goliath stood in frunt of Israelite armies an sed "Whai dont yu coem out an fight? I am sweet champyun dood but yu guyz ar teh suckz. Yu chuz wun of ur army kittehs to coem an fite wif me. **8** If he winz, Iz makes yu awl cheezburgers an cookiez an Iz wont evun eet dem. But if I winz,

yu has to maek me cheezburgers an cookies wifout evun eetin dem. K? **10** Cuz, srsly, Iz dont fink yu guyz can do it cuz yu jus suk dat much. Srsly." **11** Wen Saul an teh Israelite kittehs herd dis dey got reel scardey an peed der pantz.

16 An fer fowty dayz an nitez Goliath strut in front ov teh Israelite army.

17 Den wun day Jesse sez, "Oh hai David. Take dis fud to ur brotherz. **18** An heer is a cheezburger fer der captain. Maek sure ur bros ar ok an den coem home an tellz me wut dey ar doin. Kthnxbai." **19** Cuz David bros wer at teh camp at teh vally to fite teh Philistine kittehs.

20 So David told othur kitteh to wach aftur teh sheep an he left fer teh camp wif teh fud jus as his daddy sed cuz he wus gud kitteh. He got der jus as teh armys wer gettin reddy to do teh fite stuff or sumfing. **21** Teh two armys faec each othur. **22** David gaev teh fud to teh supply keep an wen to go see his bros. **23** As he wer talken to his bros, teh big meen Goliath caem owt to see wut teh Israelite kittehs wer doin. He start to teez dem, liek yusual.

24 As soon as teh Israelite army saw teh Goliath, dey ran away an hied. **25** "Has yu seen dat giant?" teh kittehs ask, "He coem owt evri day to laff at us. Teh King has offured lotz of cheezburgers to gif to teh kitteh who can maek teh Goliath ded. He wil evun giv dat man his awsum sexxi dotter an he wuldnt evur haf to pay teh tax agen!"

31 Dem soem kitteh told teh King Saul dat David wuz askin qweshtun an teh King Saul ask to see David becus he wanted to see him.

32 "Dont yu worry bowt dis stoopid Philistine kitteh," David sed to teh King, "Iz go an fite him fer yu. Srsly. Kthnxbai."

33 "Dont has teh stoopid!" sed King Saul, "No wai can yu fite dis Philistine kitteh an win. No wai. Ur littul kitten an he is big strong kitteh. He has ben fiter since he kitten. So jus no wai, dood, no wai."

34 But David sed, "Wai. Iz can beat him. Iz ben takin caer ov mah daddyz aminals an stuff an dis wun tiem a lyon caem an try to steel wun to maek cheezburger wif, **35** An Iz maek it ded. Srsly. Iz beat it wif a club an broek his jaw an stuff. **36** Iz will do dat to dis Philistine kitteh cuz he maek fun uv teh army of teh Ceiling Cat! **37** Ceiling Cat saev meh frum teh lyon, he will so saev meh frum teh Goliath. So wai. Srsly."

An den King Saul sed, "K. may Ceiling Cat be wif yu!"

38 Saul gaev David sum uv his armor. He gaev a reely sweet helmet an stuff. **39** David try it on an walkd arownd in it for a sec cuz he nevur wear wun befor.

"No wai can Iz wear dis. I no used to it. Do not want." So David tuk it off. **40** So he wen to teh river an got five rocks. An den wif only hiz rockz an hiz walkn stik he wen to teh vally to fite teh Goliath.

41 Goliath walk owt to see David **42** An laffed at him **43** "Srsly, lil kittem, am Iz liek sum dog dat yu try to beat me up wif a stik? Srsly dood, dat is teh suck. **44** Coem heer an see me so Iz can grownd yu up lek berdy fud!" Goliath yelled.

45 An David sed, "Yu coem to me wif awl ur fancy armys an stuff, but Iz coem to yu in teh naem of Ceiling Cat an his armys, yu kno, Ceiling Catz armys dat yu liek to teez so much. **46** Today, Ceiling Cat wil totaly taek yu, an Iz so goin to kill yu an cutz off ur hed an stuff. An den, Iz will grownd awl ur armys liek berdy fud. Den evriwun will kno dat Ceiling Cat lives in israel! **47** An evriwun heer wil kno dat Ceiling Cat saev his kittehs an he dont evun need any ov dat fancy armor stuff. Dis is totaly Ceiling Cat's battul an he will so gif yu to me. Kthnx."

48 So Goliath caem forwurd to meet David an David ran at him. **49** He grab wun of hiz rocks an den he liek frew it at Goliath! An teh rock hit Goliath in teh hed an he fell ovur an wus ded. Pwnd!

50 So David so totaly beat teh Goliath wif jus a rock! He no evun has a sword or nething! **51** He taek Goliath's sword an cut off Goliath's hed.

Wen teh Philistine armys saw dat der big awsum champyum wus ded dey ran away. **52** Den teh Israel an Judah kittehs yell, "Yay! We rockz! We has teh awsum!" an chase aftur teh Philistines. **53** Den dey wen bak to teh Philistine camp an steal awl der cheezburgers an stuff. **54** (David tuk teh Goliath's hed to Jerusalem, but he put teh Goliath's sweet armur in his tent. Srsly.)

Elisha Git Maed Fun ov... fer teh Last Tiem

23 An Elisha wus goin up to Bethel. An as he wus walkin deez kittens coem owt an dey maek fun of Elisha cuz he wus missin his wiskurs. An dey laff at hiem an go, "Go to teh Ceiling No-Whiskurs. Go up to teh Ceiling No-Whiskurs! LOL. Yu luk funni." **24** Den he gif dem teh evul eye an curse at dem in teh naem of Ceiling Cat. Den oh noes! Deez two reely big bearz coem owt of teh woods an nom awl teh kittehs ded. Dey totawly got pwned. Srsly. **25** An den Elisha go to Samaria insted, cuz he forgetz whar he wus goin.

Ceiling Cat Be Mah Shepherd

Psalm 23

1 Ceiling Cat is mai sheperd. He gif me evrithing Iz need.

2 He letz me sleeps in teh sunni spot an has liek nice watterz ovar thar.

3 He maek mai soul happehan maek sure Iz go teh riet wai for him. Liek thru teh cat flap insted of owt teh open windo, LOL.

4 Iz in teh vally of dogz, fearin no pooch, becuz Ceiling Cat iz besied me rubbin mah ears, an it maek me so kumfy.

5 He letz me sit at teh tabul evun wen peepul who no liek me iz watchin. He gifs me a flea baff an so much gooshy fud it runz out ov mai bowl, LOL.

6 Niec tings an luck wil chase me evridayan Iz will liv in teh Ceiling Cats howse forevur

Ceiling Cat is mai shepherd.

He gif me evrithing Iz need.

Let him kiss me wif teh kissus ov iz mouf.

Song ov Solomon

Song of Songs 1

Solomones Song of Songz, kthx.

Teh Beluved:

2 Let him kiss me wif teh kissus ov iz mouf. Iz loev his mouf kissus-- for ur loev be moar delitefool den cheezbugerz. Srsly, Iz Pwnz!

3 Yu has a flavur Iz liek; yer naem is liek smellz poorded owt. Deh oter chikz loev yu too!

4 Taek me wif yu pleez, coem on! Letz go! Teh King bring me into hiz chamburz, k?

Teh Friendz:

We liekz yu, k? We delitez yu, we wil praiz ur loev moar den cheezburgers, rly!

Teh Beluved:

Iz loev yu!

5 I am teh dark, but i be purdy. Oh dotters ov Jerusalem dark liek teh couches of Kedar, liek chocolat, liek teh curtains of Solomon dat Iz climez awl day.

6 Do no stare at me cus Iz witch color, becuz Iz darkened by dat big brite ballz ov teh warminess Iz lay in. Dat jus mean. no rly, stop staring! Mai bros beez angry wif me cuz I am a gurl. day no like gurl kittehs an maed me do werk in teh vineyards, but dey maed me not put sunskreen on. Dey wuz mean.

7 Hey yu! Yeh, teh wun I loev, whar yu graze yur flockz and whar yu bring yer lazy sheepz at lunch tiem. Why shud Iz be liek teh siamcats? necks to teh flockz of ur friendz?

Teh Friendz:

8 Ur pritty so we halped yu. If yu dunt know follow teh poop trailz of teh sheepz an graze yer yung goats by teh tents of teh shephurdz.

Teh Luver:

9 Ur liek teh horse. Wait, no! Liek... liek teh wunz on teh cheryits of Pharo. Wait... Iz sory.

10 Ur cheekz are teh shiny wif shiny tingz like pomehgranitz. Ur

neck is wif strings of jewelz, en I plays wif dem.

11 We will maek yu teh earringz of teh gohld wif silver studz.

Teh Beluved:

12 Whiel teh King wuz at his tabul eating cheezburgerz, my smellz go owt.

13 My luver be liek teh sack ov catnip I put between mah brests. Iz want him der.

14 My luver be liek teh clusterz of henna blossumz frum teh vineyardz of En Gedi.

Teh Luver:

15 Ur teh beautifool! Darlin! Oh, yu are teh beautifool! Ur eyez be liek littul small durty berdz. I wants to eet dem!

Teh Beluved:

16 Ur teh handsum, mah luver! An ur charmin. Our green bed be teh virgin!

Teh Luver:

17 Teh beemz of our houz be cedarz an our roofthings are ferz.

Song of Songs 8

Teh Beluved:

1 I wish yu wer mai bro,so we cud hav hawt cestuous makeowtsin frunt of ppl.dats nawt weird, iz it?

2 Plus we cud be in saem howse,drinkin mai winez an joose an cookies.

3 hugz!

4 but srsly, dotters of Jerusalem, dun waek loev up early, ok?It ar cranky laet sleeper kthx.

Teh Friendz:

5 Who is in our dezertleanin on boyfren kittehs?

Teh Beluved

No in dezert silly. Iz undur apple tree.ur mom lieks apple tree too. is very populer tree.lots of babies borning an stuff.dey shud cleen der moar. **6** i has a bukkit.bukkit is ur hart.bukkit is awlso on fier an ded an stuffs.but iz stil gud bukkit. **7** Loev gets put in sink but is no drownded.awlso yu cant buy it, sory.

Teh Friendz:

8 Ok, so liek we haf dis sisturWho is no growned up an sexy yet.wut do we do wif sistur? **9** We dress her up all pertyan maek lolicon fer internets!

Teh Beluved:

10 Who care? Iz has boobies. boyfren lieks dem. **11** Solomon has a vinyard in sum hard to spel plaec.Tenants can has Solomon's vinyard.he gets money wen frootz get eeted. **12** Iz has a vinyard too!Solomon can has mai vinyard an money.he is gud boyfren kitteh. Guys dat tend teh vinyard get mones too Iz gess.

Teh Luver:

13 wai yu spendin all ur tiemin garden wif frenz?I can has ur voice?Iz mean nawt liek takin ur actual voice or nething but, liek, talkin an singing an stuffs. Yodeling be ok awlso.

Teh Beluved:

14 Ok lets go to mowntensan be deers an gazeles

Teh Story ov Job

Job 1

1 In teh land of Uz wuz a man calded Job. Teh man wuz gud, wif respeck fer teh Ceiling Cat an haet teh evilz. **2** Teh man hadz seven sunz and tree doters, **3** An lots of mices an camlez an rinoceruseses an servnts an stuff. Srsly. **4** His sunz tuk turns maekin cookies, an they all eated them. **5** And Job wuz liek "Oh noes! Wut if cookies were sin? Gota prai, jus in caes."

Furst Tess

6 Teh angulz wented to seez Ceiling Cat, an Basement Cat wented awlso. **7** Ceiling Cat sez to Basement Cat, "Whar wuz yu?" Basement Cat sez bak, "Oh, hai. I wuz in ur urfs, walkin up an down uponz it." **8** Teh Ceiling Cat sez, "Has yu seen mai servunt Job? He can has cheezburger cuz he laiks me."

9 "No wai!" sed Basement Cat. **10** "Yu jus playin favrits. **11** If yu taek his cheezburgers, or his bukkit, he no laiks yu no moar."

12 Den teh Ceiling Cat sez, "Okai, yu can taek his bukkit, but no givin Job owies." An den Basement Cat went awai.

13 Wun day Job's sunz an doters were eatin cookiez at teh oldest wuns howse, **14** An a kitteh caem to told Job a messuj. "Yer donkiez an moo-cows was eateding tasteh grass **15** An den bad kittehs were in yer hous killin yer dudez an yer aminals got stold an only I gotz awai."

16 An den anotter kitteh caem to told Job a diffrant messuj. He sez, "Teh Ceiling Cat maed hot fier fawl frum teh Ceiling an it burnd up yer sheepz an moar servunts an onli I gotz awai."

17 An den a moar diffrunter kitteh caem an told Job a messuj, "Sum angry dudez tuk yer rinoceroseseses an kill moar servunts an only i gotz awai."

18 An den wun moar kitteh caem to Job wif a messuj. **19** "Yer sunz howse feld ovur an skwishded evryones. Srry."

20 Den Job got up andshaved an wus liek, "Gota prai nao."

21 "Teh Ceiling Cat giv me cheezburger, teh Ceiling Cat taek mah cheezburger awai. I stil laiks teh Ceiling Cat."

22 Job prai to Ceiling Cat an didnt afraid of anyone. Do want.

Job 2

1 On a diffrunt day moar Anguls caem an prezent demselfs befoar Ceiling Cat, an Basement Cat caem fer giggulz. **2** An Ceiling Cat sez to Basement Cat, "Whar wer yu?" Basement Cat sez bak to Ceiling Cat, "Im in ur urfz, walkin up and down uponz it. Did I tell yu dis befor?" An Ceiling Cat wuz like, "Oh yeah, sry" an Basement Cat said, "It ok."

3 Den Ceiling Cat sez to Basement Cat, "Has yu seen mai servunt Job? He can has cheezburger cuz he laiks me stil en he hatez yu still, even tho yu eated all hiz cookiez an killeded hiz servnts an stuff wif no reesons. Haha!"

4 "Cookiez for cookiez!" Basement Cat sed bak. "Anee kitteh wil gif awl fer hiz own lifez **5** I betz if yu hitz his body an boneses he gunna curse yu ugly faec."

6 Ceiling Cat den say, "Ok, he iz yers. Jus dun maek him ded, dat be bad."

7 Basement Cat went owt to deh Urfs an gaev Job teh herpiez awl ovur hiz body, even on hiz paws an head. **8** Job wuz nazty en he scrapeded off hiz sores an eat dem.

9 Job's wief sed to him, "OMG. Curse teh Ceiling Cat an get dead, stoopid."

10 An Job wuz like, "OMG, yu ar stoopid. We accept cookiez frum Ceiling Cat but dunt let him taek teh cookiez away? Why dun yu jus go awayz!" Job did nawt invisibul error teh whoel tiem!

11 Den Job's tree frendz, der namez wer Eliphaz, Bildad, an Zophar, herd bout awl teh problumz dat Job has an dey went away frum der homez an met an dey coem to maek Job feelz bettur. **12** Wen dey saw Job dey saweded that he luk very ugliez an dey sez, "Hoo diz ugli womanz?" an den dey saw it wus Job an dey criez an stuffz. Den dey got nakedz for som reeson but I dun kno wai. **13** Den tey got down onto the groundz wif Job and staid wif him fer seven days and seven nitez an they did no speeks, becuz dey saw how big Job suferin wuz.

Job 3

1 Den aftur diz Job open hiz mouf an curse teh day he caem out of hiz mommiez.

2 He sez:**3** "I hoep teh day I wus born jus go awayz, and teh nite it wuz say, 'I has a girl! Wait, I wuz wrong, I has a boy!' **4** An I hopes Dr. Brown goez back to teh pasts an turns off teh lites, **5** cuz Ceiling Cat dont care. **6** An I hopes the littul kittehs get into

teh calanders an stealz awl the Caturdayz. **7** Look, I beez emo. **8** I tink we shud waek up teh lolrus, an steelz his bukkit. **9** An I haet teh sunz!

10 Wen I wus bornz, dey say, 'Wun kitteh, two kitteh, tree kitteh, four kitteh.'" **11** Dey shud sed, "Wun kitteh, two kitteh, tree kitteh, ded kitteh!" **12** Ded kittehs dont drinks the milk. **13** They liv in shoes bokses, **14** with the lulz **15** an cheezburgers. **16** Sleeping cat sleepz in teh bokses. **17** Ded cat jus sleepz in teh littel bokses. **18** Teh kittehs that sayz "'Halp!' can has cheezburgerz?" **19** Teh littel kittehs an teh diabeetus kitteh is there.

20 Turnz off teh lites! **21** I no can has cheezburgerz? **22** Then I dont wants ur cheezburgerz!

23 Ceiling Cat stold mai internets **24** an I sayd 'halp!' **25** Now I iz emo, **26** an no has cheezburgers."

Teh Writin on teh Wall

Daniel 5

1 King Belshazzar gaev fud to liek tons of his favrit kittehs. **2** An den teh King want soem shinee cups dat he stoel frum teh Tempul of Ceiling Cat so dat he an his wifes cud drink frum dem. **3** An dey drank an drank. **4** An dey laff abowt Ceiling Cat an pray to not reel sky kittehs ov silvur an gowld. DO NOT WANT!

5 Den OH NOES! A big paw apeer in thin air, jus liek dat! An teh King wach it wriet on teh wall. **6** An teh scaredy cat King lef a puddul undur him cuz he wus so scaredy.

7 An teh King meows owt to awl teh majik kittehs, teh star reeders, an he sez to deez smrat kittehs of Babylon, "Anywun who can has reedin dis writin, an tell me wat it sez, yu gunna get gowld an Iz gunna maek yu a rooler. Srsly!

8 An awl ov teh smart kittehs no kno wat teh writin sez. **9** An teh King wuz evun moar scareded. An teh nobels were liek, "WTF?"

10 Teh queen herd awl ov tis an go to see wut goin in. She coem in an sez, "King! Yu lif furevar. Srsly! No be fraidy cat! Yu can has pried! **11** I kno dis kitteh hoo reel smart, an he is a man hoo yer fadder lieked. He maed him top majic kitteh! **12** Teh kitteh be naemed Daniel, but teh King call him Belteshazzar, cuz he wuz crazee. An dis guy, he reely can halp yu. He kno hao to get messuges frum dreemz an stuffz. He kno what dis say."

13 An dey woek Daniel up and browt him to teh King, an teh King sez, "Ar yu Daniel? **14** I herd yu ar wun smart kitteh! **15** My odder majic kittehs, dey nawt so smart. Dey no can reed teh writin on teh wall! **16** I herd yu reel gud at dis stuff. So if yu can rede teh writin on teh wall, iz gunna gif yu lotz of cheezburgers an belleh rubz. An yu gunna be teh numba three kitteh in teh kingdom. Srsly."

17 Daniel sez bak, "DO NOT WANT. Iz jus tell yu wat it meenz, an I go bak to mah napz."

18 "Ceiling Cat gif yer fadder Nebuchadnezzar lotz of cheezburgers an gud stuffz, srsly. **19** Yu gif him high posishunz, an kittehs feer him, srsly. An he did watever he wantz. He cud maek kittehs ded if he want dem ded. He cud maek kittehs rich an por. **20** But den teh King get big hed an he go bai bai. **21** He go awai an he start actin liek a moocow, eating teh gras an lettin teh mornin dewe go on him. Ceiling Cat is teh best, srsly, an he shud kno dis.

22 "Yu ar his son, but yu kno maek yerself humbul. Srsly. Belshazzar, whai yu so stoopid? **23** Yu tryin to do battul. Yu wer in his tempulz, stealin teh cups. An yu let everiwun yu liek drink frum dem. Yu wership teh kittehs of gowld and silvur. But dey no reel! Yu no wership Ceiling Cat, an dat bad! **24** So dat is whai dis paw wriet on teh wall.

25 "Dis is wut teh wall sez.: Mene , Mene , Tekel , Parsin

26 "Wut dat meen, yu say? It meen dis: Mene : Ceiling Cat sez yu no rool anymoar.

27 Tekel : Ceiling Cat put yu on scalez, an yu nawt to gret, srsly.

28 Peres : Yer kingdum gunna be split wif teh Medes an Persians."

29 Den Belshazzar's maek Daniel put on niec cloths, awl purpul, an put cheezburgers on his tabel. He evun maed Daniel teh thurd gretest kitteh in teh kingdum.

30 Belshazzar, king ov teh Babylonians, wuz maed ded. **31** an Darius teh Mede tuk ovur teh kingdum, wen he wuz owld, sicksty-too.

Daniel an teh Pooch's Den

Daniel 6

1 Darius teh Mede sez, "I can has 120 provinsus?" An he get dem. An he maek a kitteh rooler ovur every wun of dem. Srsly. **2** Den he maek Daniel an two othur kittehs big top cat to protekt teh King shinee tings an cheezburgers. **3** Daniel wus so gud at his job dat teh king thawt dat he cud wun day be top cat of teh entiyur empier. Srsly.

6 So awl teh top cats go rownd to teh king an dey sez, "Oh king, yu can has liev furevur, srsly." **7** An awl ov teh top cats agree dat teh king shud tell awl teh othur kittehs to wership him. Ani kitteh hoo do nawt want to wership teh king fer teh necks thurty dayz shud be thrown into teh pooch's den, whar awl teh scaree pooches be kept. **8** Dey sez, "Oh hai. Yu shud put dis in writin so dat awl teh kittehs kno hoo be boss an so dat nobodi can sez, 'Oh but I no kno what yu sez. Sry.'" **9** So King Darius put it in writin so

dat kittehs can has no problums knowin teh law.

10 Wen Daniel herd bowt teh decree he dun caer an go hoem an pray jus liek he alwais dus. He pray by teh windowz dat wer opun poynted to Jerusalem. He did dis tree tiems a day cuz he was totawly kewl liek dat, srsly. **11** Den a groop of kittehs go rownd to Daniel an see him praying. It a trap! **12** Teh groop of kittehs go to teh king an dey tattul on Daniel liek whinee littul kittens: "Did yu wriet down law sayin dat kittehs must wership yu fer teh necks thurty dayz? An did yu wriet dat ani kitteh hoo no folowz dis rool get totawly pwned in teh pooch den?" Teh King sez, "Whai yes. Dat troo. an teh law can no be chanjed nao, dat wud luk bad. Srsly."

13 Den teh groop of kittehs tink to demselfs, "Woot" cuz teh trap be set. An den dey sez to teh King, "Oh looki heer, Daniel no prai to yu. He pray to Ceiling

Cat insted an no pay attenshun to yu. He shud be pwned fer dis." 14 Teh king herd dis an he no happeh at awl, cuz he liek Daniel lotz. So he triez to saev him til teh sun go down.

15 Den the kittehs poek at teh King agin an sez to him, "Remebur King, yu no can brek a rool dat yu maek. Dat be aginst teh biggur law. So yu has to do wut yu sez yu do in teh law."

16 So teh King gif teh ordur an kittehs go an git Daniel an thro him in teh Pooch's Den. An teh King luk at Daniel an sez, "Dood. I hoep Ceiling Cat can protekt yu, cuz yu gunna git pwned. Srsly."

17 An dey put a big hevy rok ovur teh mouf of teh den so dat Daniel no has escaeps. An teh king put his paw on teh rok an maek a sign so dat Daniel can no has no governur pardun. **18** Den teh king go bak hoem an he wus so sad he eet no cheezburgers. He dun evun play wif his XBocks, dat hao sad he wuz. He tri to taek cat nap but he no get no slepe.

19 Tehnecks day teh King rush to teh Pooch's Den an luk fer Daniel down it. **20** He luk down in teh den an cawl down wif a scardee mew an he sez, "Daniel. Yu der. Did Ceiling Cat maek teh poochies no eet yu?"

21 Daniel meow bak up, "Oh hai. Iz in yer den. pettin yer poochies. 22 Ceiling Cat sent dis HovrCat to shut teh moufs ov teh poochies so dat dey no eet meh. Ceiling Cat tinks I am reely kewl an stuffz. I nawt evun do bad tings to yu, eithur.

23 Teh King sez, "Woot!" an ordur Daniel to be takin owt ov teh den. An dey luk ovur Daniel an der wer no cutz or scraches. Ceiling Cat halp Daniel cuz Daniel alwais trust in Ceiling Cat.

24 Den teh King gifs ordurs fer teh groop of kittehs hoo lie bowt Daniel to be put in teh den. He evun maek der wifez an kittens get thrown in teh den too, wich is kind ov meen cuz dey no do no bad tings at awl, but teh King was prolly jus reely reely mad. An as teh kittehs fawl into teh den teh

So teh King gif teh ordur an kittehs go an git Daniel an thro him in teh Pooch's Den.

poochies jump up an eet dem awl ded. Srsly. Dey got pwned.

25 Den King Darius wriet owt anothur law to awl teh kittehs ov teh land an it sez, "Liev long an prospur. Srsly.

26 "Nao lissun to meh. I kno I say wership meh, but dat jus stoopid. Yu shud wership Ceiling Cat, teh God Kitteh ov Daniel. "Cuz Ceiling Cat is so leet an he go on ferevur liek Long Cat; his howse no git distroyed, an

he gunna pwn fer a veri veri long tiem.

27 Ceiling Cat taekez in strayz an saevs kittehs; an he do deez awsum triks in teh ceiling an in teh urfz. He evun halp Daniel an maek sure dat Daniel no maek ded by pooch."

28 So Daniel liev long an prospur frum Darius to teh othur King, Cyrus, hoo wus a Persian kitteh.

Jonah an teh Big Fishie

Jonah 1

1 Wun tiem, Ceiling Cat sez to Jonah, **2** "Yu goes to Nineveh. Tellz tehm, Ceiling Cat sez "Oh I see wat yu did tehre. DO NOT WANT! Doom on yu! kthnxbai." **3** But Jonah packs hiz bukkits and flee to Joppa and buy tikkits to Spain.

4 Den Ceiling Cat haz maked wind, an maeked a sobad storm coem up. Teh ROFLcopter was neerly broken to pieces. **5** Teh sailors wuz fraidys. Tehy all skeered and preying to invisibul manz cuz kittehs do nawt liek to get wet. Dey even tossen teh cookies ovurbord fer bettar floatin. Awl dis tiem, Jonah is loafin, an sez "Fiev moar minits plz.". **6** Teh ROFLcaptin sez, "Excuze me. Wat yu sleeping fer? Get up an pray to yer invisibul man yu wuz tellin us abowt! Maybi he will not maek us ded. Maybi he sends uz saef to ar forevar home."

7 Teh sailors aks der invisibul mans who started it. Srsly. An der invisibul mans pwnz Jonah. Den dey makez a gang and poek Jonah, cuz it hiz fault. **8** Dey akses him, "Whai yu starting dis? Who maek winds? Is not sew grate akshully. Is yu in teh seawerker union? Where iz yer cheezburger? Who are yr forevar fambly?" **9** Jonah sez, "Oh hai. Is okay. Sry I skare yu. I haz harbl, an Ceiling Cat wat creayted heavun an urfs an stuff an not eeted it, is mai homeboi." **10** Den, dey start cryin an howlin, cuz Jonah alredy teld dem hiz camoflage iz no werkin. Den dey sez, "Orly? Ceiling Cat knows all an seez all. Yu broked it. Srsly."

11 Teh storm kept wavin. Iz microwave, den mexican wave. **12** Jonah sez "Resistince iz fewtile. Biff me in teh sea, oshun can pwnz kitteh. Is mai fawlt. Sry." **13** But Michael triez to row teh boat to shoer. He is fail, an teh storm iz getting wors an wors. **14**

So dey prai to Ceiling Cat, "Wait. no! Plz no drowns us, cuz cats dus no lieks to get wet. DO NOT WANT. Kthnxbai." **15** Den dey toss Jonah into teh waterz, and teh sea is calmed down liek on ritlin. Srsly. **16** Teh sailors iz so skeered dey maekes offrings of catnips an cheezeburgers an loots in bukkits fer Ceiling Cat. **17** Ceiling Cat maeked a LOLrus to eated Jonah, an Jonah iz in yer whale making yer sushis for three days an three nites.

Jonah 2

1 Jonah prai to Ceiling Cat frum insied teh big fish **2** An sed, "Becuz I is so veri upset, I call fer teh Ceiling Cat, an he heer me. Evun frum teh deep bad wet plais I callz, an yu heer me.

3 Fer yu throwz me into teh nasti watter, an maek me wet all ovur, wif yer waevs an splashus. **4** I sed, 'Im out of yer siet, lookn at yer holey tempul'. **5** Teh watter all rownd me, maek me wet riet thru: I got seaweedz all rownd mah hed. **6** I sink down riet to mowntans roots, I thinkin I iz traped beneef teh urfs ferevur. Oh noes! But yu rescew me aliev frum teh hole, Ceiling Cat.

7 I goin to die. Oh noes! But jus den I remembur teh Ceiling Cat, an I prai to yer holi tempul. **8** I rong to fix clawz into wrong tingz, no cheezburgr for teh bad kitteh. **9** But nao I singin happi songz and I pay yu bak fer yer halp jus liek I sez. Kitteh-savng iz doen by teh Ceiling Cat."

10 So den teh Ceiling Cat speke to big fish an it barf up Jonah on teh shoer.

Jonah 3

1 Den Ceiling Cat look down frum hoel in teh ceiling agin an sez to Jonah: **2** "Oh hai. Go to Nineveh and howl and youwl an tell dem dis trufs."

3 An Jonah did what Ceiling Cat sez fer him to do dis tiem, cuz kittehs DO NOT WANT gettin wet. Nao Nineveh is a srsly big citti. It taek liek three days to go der. Srsly. **4** On teh furst day, Jonah go into teh citti. He yowls,

"Forti maor days an Nineveh will haf no cheezburger. Invisibul Anvil is coming! Ceiling Cat is gunna pwnz yu. HAHA!"

5 Wait! No! Teh Ninevites beleef Ceiling Cat. Dey put down der cheezburgers an teh pokemans, evun teh Charizards. **6** Wen teh king of Nineveh heer dis, he tuk off his roebs, an lay down nekkid in teh dust. Oh noes! **7** Den he sez "OMGWTFBBQ! Nineveh, no let kittehs or aminals or burdies or fishz or maor livin stuff has a flavur. DO NO WANT. Srsly." **8** So teh kittehs an aminals an hoomins hied in yer dirteh cloths bukkitz an praid. **9** Who knew? Ceiling Cat miet tink dat gud enuf an not eatz us or maek us ded." **10** Wen Ceiling Cat see wat dey did der he calls it Caturday an gived dem cheezburgers an cookies.

Jonah 4

1 Jonah got mad tho. He wuz lookin forwerd to seein teh Ninevites get pwnd an sayin "I told yu so." **2** He wuz liek "Ceiling Cat, yu is niec. **3** So plz kil me nao kthnxbai." **4** But Ceiling Cat wuz liek "DO NOT WANT!"

5 Jonah sit down to see wat happun to teh citti. **6** Ceiling Cat maeded a plant gro, an teh shaed maeded Jonah happi. **7** But teh nekst mornin Ceiling Cat send a wurm an it eated teh plant. **8** An Ceiling Cat maed teh sun shien so briet dat Jonah want to die agin.

9 Ceiling Cat wuz liek "Why yu is mad about teh plant?" Jonah wuz liek "STFU, dat plant wuz makin me happi, yu suk." **10** Ceiling Cat wuz all "Yu caer abowt teh plant evun tho yu do nuffin fer it an evun tho it wuz onli heer fer a dai. **11** But teh citti of Niniveh haz lotz of kittehs. Shud I caer about it?"

Happy Cat is Born

Luke 1

26 Ceiling Cat sended Gabriowl, a hovur kitteh, to Nazareth (dat is a citti in Galilee) **27** to a virgun naemed Mary. She wuz engajed to a kitteh naemed Joseph. **28** Gabriowl wuz liek "O hai Mary, yu iz realli nice. Ceiling Cat is wif yu." **29** Mary wuz kiend of worrid abowt dat. **30** But teh hovur kitteh wuz all, "Do nawt be fraid. Ceiling Cat is happi wif yu. **31** Yu is gunna haf a kittun. Naem him Happy Cat. **32** He wil be graet. He wil be teh kittun of Ceiling Cat an his daddi will gif him David's chaer. **33** He wil rool Jacob's howse forevur."

34 Mary wuz liek, "O rly, I is a virgn remembur." **35** Gabriowl wuz all, "Ceiling Cat wil taek caer of it." **36** Elizabeth iz goin to haf a kittun an evribodi sed it wuz imposibul." **37** Nothin is imposibul fer Ceiling Cat."

38 Mary sed, "I happi to do Ceiling Cat's werk. Liek yu sai." An Gabriowl lefted.

41 Wen Elizabeth hurd dat, teh kittun insied her gotted all excieted. **42** Elizabeth wuz all, "Ceiling Cat gifs yu cheezburger, an he gif ur kittun cheezburger too. **43** I is lucki dat teh mothur of mai Lord coem to see me. **44** Jus luk at wat mai kittun did wen he heared yu. **45** If yu beleev dat wat Ceiling Cat sed to yu wil coem true, yu can haz cheezburger."

46 Mary sed, "Ceiling Cat is laik a big deal, **47** I is happy abowt Ceiling Cat... **48** becuz he kepted me in maind an nao evribodi knowz i can haz cheezburger. **49** Tank yu Ceiling Cat, yu is cool. **50** Yu is niec to evribodi. **51** Cept kittehs who do nawt diserv it, LOL. **52** Yu has pwned teh roolurzwhiel stil bein niec to teh noobz. **53** Yu gif cookies to teh hungriwhiel yu tolded teh rich "Niec trai." **54** Yu wuz niec to Israel **55** an to all Abraham's famili liek yu promis."

56 Mary stay wif Elizabeth three munfz. Den she wented hoam.

Luke 2

1 Roun dis tiem, Caesar Augustus wuz like, "I can has cenzus?" **2** (Coz while Quirinius was Teh Boz of Syria, is invisibul census!) **3** And all teh doodz went home for teh saying, "I is heer!" **4** So Joseph went frum Nazareth to Judeah to Bethlehem whar David wuz borned, coz David wuz hiz graete-graete gran-daddie, **5** An Mary went wif him, coz she was gonna be married wif him an she was preggerz. **6** Wen wuz tiem for teh baybee, **7** it wuz a boy, so he wuz wrapd in blanket like burrito an placd him in fud dish, cuz innkeeper wuz liek, "No room heer, kthxbye!"

8 Den der wuz sheep-doods in teh feeld, an dey wuz watchin teh sheep in teh dark. Is very very boring. Srsly. **9** An suddenly, visibul angel! An glory! O noez!! **10** But teh angel sed, "Is ok, yu can has gud news for awl teh doodz! **11** Todai in da city ov David, you can has sayvur! Is Christ teh Lord! W00t! **12** Is sign fer yu, find da baybee wrapd like brrito in a big fud dish." **13** An suddenly, moar angelz! Dey sez, **14** "W00t to teh Ceiling Cat! An cheezburgers fer doodz he luffs! Kthxbai."

15 An wen teh angelz go invisibul agin, sheep-doodz sed, "Sweet, nao we find teh brrito-baybee sayvur!" **16** So dey left da sheeps (sheeps ar vry borng) and found Joe an Mary and da baybee in da fud dish. **17** An when dey saw it wuz baybee an not brrito, they told evrywun he wuz kewl, **18** An all teh doodz who herd were lyke, "neat-o brrito!" **19** An Mary wuz lyke, "o rly?" **20** Teh sheep-doodz sed, "Yay fer Ceiling Cat! Was not invisible brrito!" **21** On dai noomber ate, it wuz tiem to circumcize him (iz laik getting fixd) an they called him Happy Cat, 'coz teh angel sed tht wuz hiz name

An when dey saw it wuz **baybee** an not **brrito**, they told evrywun he wuz **kewl**.

John teh Baptist

Luke 1

5 Wen Herrod had cheezburgers, sum dood callz Zechariah hads waif callz Liz. **6** Dey laiks Ceiling Cat an does not pee on his rug. **7** But dey wuz old an still has no kittens. **8** Wun day, Zechariah waz serving Ceiling Cat, **9** he hadz to smoke da catnip **10** wen every doodz was preying. **11** An der was an angel in teh catnip - **12** O noez! **13** But teh angel sed "Is ok. Yu can has a kitteh. Calls him Jon. **14** You can has partiez an all teh doodz also, **15** For Ceiling Cat will laik him; but he cans not has da drinkies. **16** An he will work for teh Ceiling Cat **17** and maek awl teh doodz sry dey wus bad." **18** An Zechariah sed: "Wat? But me and mai waif has rinkles" **19** An teh angel sed, "Srsly, Iz Gabriowl. I kno Ceiling Cat, who sendz me, **20** But 'cos you doesn't beleev me you can has no voice for now. Kthxbai".

21 Evrybodi wondur whai Zechariah wuz takin so long in teh tempul. **22** Wen he coem owt he cud no talk. But evrybodi figur owt he hadded a visiun, becuz he act it owt. **23** Evenchly his tour of duti wuz up an he coem hoem. **24** An hiz wief Elizabeth got pregnant. **25** "Tank yu Ceiling Cat," she sed.

57 Elizabeth's kittun wuz a boi. **58** Evrybodi wuz happi. **59** Dey had his boi-harbls fixed (but not liek ur thinkin). Dey wus gonna naem him Zechariah, **60** but Elizabeth wus awl "STFU we iz callin him John."

61 Evrybodi wus awl "No wai." **62** Dey tried to figur owt wat Zechariah want to call him. Zechariah cud no talk, remembur? **63** He rited down, "John." Evrybodi wus liek "OMG srsly?" **64** As soon as dat happun he cud talk agin an he wuz awl, "Tanks Ceiling Cat." **65** Evrybodi wus awl "OMG." **66** An dey wundur wat Ceiling Cat's plans fer John wus.

67 Hovr Cat wus in Zechariah, makin him tell teh futurez. **68** "Gud for yu Ceiling Cat, yu maed tings bettur fer Israel. **69** Yu pick up a trumpit fer us. **70** Liek teh profetz sed yu wud. **71** Yu protect us from awl teh bulliez. **72** Yu wuz niec to our daddiez an remembur dey had a deel wif yu. **73** Teh deel yu maed wif Abraham, **74** to protect us, an let us werk for yu wifout fear **75** an be gud all our lifez. **76** Mai kittun, peepulz wil cawl yu Ceiling Cat's profetbecuz we wil get evryting reddy fer him, **77** so dat peepulz Invisible Errors be forgivun, **78** becuz Ceiling Cat iz niec, liek teh sun **79** dat shienz an liets teh wai."

80 Teh kittun growd up strong evun tho he live in teh dezert

Wawter into Booze

John 2

1 On teh third dayz, soem peepulz wus gettin marriedz in Cana in teh Galilee, an Happy Cat's mom wus der. **2** Happy Cat an hiz doodz wer liek, "Weez comez awlso, lol." **3** Awl teh booze got drink, an Happy Cat's momz was liek, "Dey gotz no booze. Dis parti iz teh suck!"

4 Happy Cat sed to hiz momz, "STFU! Mai tiem iz not coem. (Burn!)"

5 But his mother wanted teh booze and telled teh doodz at teh bar,"He willz maek teh booze. Do wut he sez to do."

6 Now, der wus soem bukkitz fer washing teh selfs. Dey hold 20-30 gallonz eech.

7 Happy Cat sez, "I gots a plan. Mom wantz booze, she getz booze. Fill teh bukkitz wif wawters." And teh doodz fill dem full.

8 He sed to teh doodz, "Taek soem wawters to teh party dood." Dey did it. **9** Teh party dood wus liek, "Dis iz teh booze! I liek dis booze! Whar did dis coem frum?" (Teh doodz who brought teh booze know!) Teh party dood wentz to teh peepul gettin marriedz **10** an sed, "WTF!? Most doodz gif teh gud booze furst, an den teh crappy booze wen peepulz too drunk to caer. But dis booze pwns!"

11 Happy Cat did dis, teh furst of his signz, in Cana in teh Galilee, an revealedz his Pwnage; an Happy Cat's doodz beleefed in him.

Happy Cat an teh Leppurkitteh

Matthew 8

1 Wen he coem down frum teh mowntains, awl deez peepul caem too. **2** An den, a lepurkitteh wuz liek "O hai! Scuz me Happy Cat, I has all dees icky soerz, yu can fix PLZ?" **3** Happy Cat wuz liek "Okay kitteh. Iz fix yu." An jus liek dat he wuz all betteh. **4** But Happy Cat also wispurd one moar ting "Jus dun keep it sekrit k, go to teh cheefs an show dem."

O hai! Scuz me Happy Cat, I has all dees icky soerz, yu can fix PLZ?

STFU Storm

Matthew 8

23 Wun tiem, Happy Cat went in a boat wif his disihpawls. **24** Den awl teh sudden, dis reely reely big storm caem an wus pwning teh boat! But Happy Cat wuz jus sleepin thru dat hoel ting! **25** So his disihpawls starts shakin him an wer awl lied, "Dood! HAPPY CAT! WAEK UP! Teh ship be sinkin! We awl goin get wet, DO NOT WANT!" **26** So Happy Cat sez, "Yu get me up fer sum stoopid wind? Wut, yu tink? Iz jus gunna let yu get all wet an sink? Yu are teh noobs wif no fayf! Srsly." So Happy Cat gotz up an told the storm to shut up so he cud get sum moar sleepz. **27** Teh disihpawls wer awl liek, "Whoa! Hey guiz, didz yu see dat? Dis dood totawly pwns teh wind an evryting!"

"Dood! HAPPY CAT! WAEK UP! Teh ship be sinkin! We awl goin get wet, DO NOT WANT!"

Demunz in Piggehs

Matthew 8

28 Happy Cat finaly reach teh land He walked down deh rohd to Gadara, an two guiz wif demuns in dem jump in front of him. An dey wer awl big an tuff. 29 Den dey shoutz, "HEYOO, Almity Happy Cat, wat yu want wif us newayz? You gunna pwn us alredy?" 30 An der wer awl deez piggehs eatin over der. 31 So teh demunz sez, "Oh noes! If yu gunna pwn us, plz jus put us in teh piggehs?" 32 Happy Cat sez to dem "Okay fien. Go in teh piggehs." An teh demunz went in teh piggehs. Teh piggehs den becaem totawly emo an dey awl jump in teh laek an drownz. 33 Deez guiz hoo wer wachin wer liek "OMG!" an dey went an teld awl der frends bowt hao Happy Cat pwnd teh demunz. 34 An awl teh peepul wer totawly freekin owt an ran owt an sed to Happy Cat "Okai, heyoo guy hoo pwnd teh piggehs, DO NOT WANT. Yoo has to leav nao, srsly."

Teh Ded Dawter

Luke 8

40 Happy Cat went hoem an evriwun wuz happeh to see him. **41** Dis dood Jairus want Happy Cat to coem to hiz howse **42** becuz hiz onli dawter wuz dyin. She wuz liek twelv. So menny peepulz wantid to see Happy Cat dat teh crowdz almost crushed him. **43** Diz womun kitteh der had ben bleedin fer twelv yeerz an no wun cud help her. **44** She sneeked up behiend Happy Cat an tuched teh tip of hiz tail an she stop bleedin.

45 Happy Cat wuz liek "Ok, who didded dat?" Evribodi wuz liek, "Not me dood," an Peter wuz liek. "Itz crowdid LOL."

46 Happy Cat wuz liek, "Sumwun tuch me, Iz feel it."

47 Teh womun wuz liek, "OMG pwned," an she towld him everyting. **48** Happy Cat wuz liek,

"Yu wuz heelded becuz yu can has fayf. Yu go now."

49 Sumwun caem to tel Jairus hiz dawter wuz ded an dat he shud leav Happy Cat aloen.

50 Happy Cat wuz all, "Doan wurri, if yu beleev she wil be okay."

51 Wen Happy Cat got to Jairus' howse he wud nawt let enniwun coem in wif him. Ecksept Peter. An John an James. An Jairus an his wief of corse, it wuz der howse, LOL. **52** Evribodi wuz cryin. Happy Cat wuz all, "STFU, she jus sleepin."

53 Evribodi wuz all, "LOL noob, she has a ded." **54** But he held her paw an wuz liek "Yu can has get ups nao." **55** An she gots up!. Happy Cat wuz liek, "Giv her a cookie." **56** Her parintz wuz awl "OMG WTF," but Happy Cat tell dem nawt to tell ennibodi.

Happy Cat wuz all,
"STFU, she jus sleepin."

"Sum of dem fell in teh dirt an dey caem up an teh farmur get laytur lotz moar den he plant."

Parable ov teh Seedz

Luke 8

1 So after dat Happy Cat wented arownd doin his thing, wif hiz twelv followrz, **2** an sum ladiez too. He had heel dem frum tek icky sik stuffz. He had throwded sevun deemunz owt ov Mary Magdalene. **3** Der wuz awlso Joanna an Susanna an sum otherz. Dey wuz helpin out, supportin teh rest ov Happy Cats followrz.

4 Happy Cat tolded dis stori: **5** "A farmur went owt plantin seedz. Sum of dem fell nex to teh road. Peepulz step on dem an teh birdz nomed dem. **6** Sum of dem fel on teh rock, an wen dey coem up teh plantz drieded owt an died. **7** Sum of dem fel in teh weedz an gotted choeked. **8** Sum of dem fell in teh dirt an dey caem up an teh farmur get laytur lotz moar den he plant. So soem gud caem ov it, LOL." Wen he wuz doen wif teh stori he wuz liek, "If yu haz earz, lissun up." **9** Hiz followerz wunder wat teh stori ment. Dey at leest figur owt it wuz nawt abowt farmin, LOL. **10** He sez, "I wil let yu kno wat it meenz, but iz keepin it sekrit from teh noobz, so dat 'dey can has see an not reely see; dey can has heer an nawt undurstand, LOL.'"

11 "Here wat it meenz, k. Teh seed iz teh werd of Ceiling Cat. **12** Teh seedz bai teh paff iz teh peepul who heer, but Basement Cat coemz along an taek teh werd of Ceiling Cat out of deir hartz, so dat dey woant beleev an woant be saeved. **13** Teh wunz on teh rock iz teh peepul who heer an say, "Yay Ceiling Cat," but haz no rootz. Dey beleev fer a whiel, but wen thingz get hard dey givz up. **14** Teh wunz in teh weedz iz teh peepl who heer, but dey getz distraktid bai lief an forgitz abowt Ceiling Cat. **15** But teh wunz on teh dirt are peepulz wif gud hartz, who heer teh werd an duzint forgit.

Fiev thowsand peepulz atez.
Srsly.

Feeding teh 5,000

Mark 6

30 Teh Apawssulz caem bak, an dey tell Happy Cat awl teh stuff dey did an teech. **31** An den, becuz der wuz too many peepul an dey wuznt getting lunch, he wuz liek, "Hay, letz go rest nao, k?"

32 An so dey went away in a boat an went were nowun wuz. **33** But lotz of peepul seez dem, an chaes dem an got der furst. **34** An Happy Cat seez dem, an thawt dey wuz liek sheep wifout a shephurd. An he teech dem stuff.

35 It wuz getting laet, so teh disiples wuz liek, "Hay, itz reely laet, an we iz, liek, in teh middul of nowerez. **36** Yu sendz dem hoem so dey can noms dinnur, k?"

37 But Happy Cat wuz liek "No wai! Yu giv dem fudz!" An dey wuz liek "But dats lotz of munniez! Yu wantz us to uze dat much munniez on teh fudz?"

38 An Happy Cat wuz liek, "Hao much fudz duz we haz? Yu go check, k?" An dey checkd, an wuz liek "Der iz fiev bredz an two tunaz."

39 An den Happy Cat wuz liek, "Everiwun sitz down nao, k?" **40** An so everwun satz down on teh grass. **41** An he grabbd teh fudz, an he lukd to teh Ceiling, an wuz liek, "Hay, thx Ceiling Cat," an broek teh bredz. Den he wuz liek, "Heer, yu pass dis out, k?" **42** An everiwun ate an everwun wuz fullz, **43** an teh disiplz pick up teh leftovurz, an der wuz twelv bukkitz ful. An dey put it in teh fridge to saev fer latur. **44** Fiev thowsand peepulz atez. Srsly.

Happy Cat Walks on Wawter

Mark 6

45 An Happy Cat telled teh disiplz "Hay, yu getz in teh boat nao, k? I be dere latur." **46** An den he went on teh mountin to prai.

47 An wen it gotz all dark an stuff, teh boat wuz in teh middul of teh laek, an Happy Cat wuz aloen on teh landz. **48** An he sawz taht teh disiplz wuz rly bad at rowingz bcuz dere wuz lotz of windz. An in teh middul of teh nit, he walk owt on teh wawter, an wuz gonna pass dem, becuz he wuz reely fast, **49** but wen dey seez him, dey iz like, "OMG A GOST! WUTZ HAPPENIN?"

50 becuz dey wuz skeerd of gosts. But Happy Cat wuz liek, "Hay, Iz nawt gost! Yu no be skeerd, k?"

51 An den he got in teh boat an der wuz no wind and teh disipulz wuz amaized, **52** becuz dey didnt get wut teh majic fudz ment.

53 An dey landed at soem plaec wif a funny naem. **54** An wen dey got out of teh boat, peepul wuz like, "Hay, dats Happy Cat!" **55** An dey browt sick peepul to him on teh matz. **56** An Happy Cat heel sick peepul an stuff werever he wuz. Srsly.

Parable ov teh Niec Samaritan Dood

Luke 10

25 Den a lawyr dood aks, "Boss, hao I gits to liv forevur?" **26** Happy Cat aks, "Wut duz teh roolz say?" **27** Lawyr dood sez "Yu shud luv Ceiling Cat wif hart an soal an bodee an brainz, an yu shud luvz ur naybor as much as yu luvz urself." **28** Happy Cat sez, "Dats rite. Do dat an yu liv." **29** But lawyr dood aks, "But who beez mai naybor?"

30 Happy Cat sez "Wuns upon a tiem, a dood go frum Jerusalem to Jericho. But OH NOES! Him get beeted up an robbed an stuf, an him almost ded. Srsly! **31** Den priest dood walk by an ignor him. **32** Den Levite dood walk by an preten nawt seez him. **33** But Samaritan dood seez him and sez 'OMG! Iz yu ok?' **34** An him help hurted dood an givs him fud **35** an taekz him to vet an promis to payz vet bill.

36 So wich wun of deez tree wuz naybor to him dat got robbed?"

37 Lawyr dood sez, "Him dat wus niec to him." An Happy Cat sez, "Dats rite. So do liek dat."

Martha an Mary

Luke 10

38 Den Happy Cat goed to howse of too sistahs namd Martha an Mary. **39** An Mary sit an lissen to Happy Cat teech. **40** But Martha wuz buzi makin cookiez an cheezburgrs. An her sez,

"Happy Cat, dis hard werk! Tel Mary coem to kichen an halp me!" **41** Happy Cat sez, "Martha, chillz! LOL! **42** Lissen iz moar better den werk. We ordurz pizza or soemting."

Parable of teh Rich Dood

Luke 12

13 Den soembody sez "Boss Cat, tell mai brudder him spose to share teh inheritens wif me!" **14** Happy Cat sez, "Woah dood, dats not mai job!" **15** Den him sez, "Doan caer so much bowt stuf, cuz lief iz moar den stuf."

16 Den him sez, "Wunce upon a tiem, a rich dood had zillions of munniez. **17** An him wuz awl, 'WTF? Wher I put awl mai munniez?' **18** Den him say, 'I kno! I sel awl mai littul munny jars an get big munny jars on ebay! **19** An den I will sez, 'Woohoo doodz! PARTAY! Woot!' **20** But Ceiling Cat sez, "LOL noob! Yu git ded toniet, den who getz awl ur munniez?' **21** Dis wut happunz to noobz who keep all teh munniez an not giev anee to Ceiling Cat."

Parable ov teh Prodigal Son

Luke 15

11 Happy Cat tell dem: "Dis niec hooman had two kittehs, big kitteh an littul kitteh. **12** Littul kitteh sez, 'i can haz cheezeburger?' So da hooman gives littul kitteh cheezburger.

13 Littul kitteh goes owt and lukz for gal kittehs and does lots of buttsecks. **14** But den derz no fudz anywheres and littul kitteh want fudz. **15** So littul kitteh go to fish shop an sez, 'i can haz fishes?' **16** But no hooman luv littul kitteh. Dey evun chaes him wif broom!

17 But littul kitteh think, 'Mai hooman haz fudz an luvs kittehs. **18** I goes hoem an getz fudz an warm bed. **19** I can has cheezburger.' **20** So littul kitteh goed hoem an his hooman hug littul kitteh.

21 Littul kitteh sez, 'Can I has cheezburger nao?'

22 His hooman sez to his maidz, 'Get niec warm bed reddi fer littul kitteh nao. **23** Get cheezburger too. **24** My kitteh go away an needz fudz an bedz.'

25 Big kitteh uas playin owtside an smells cheezbuger. **26** Big kitteh aks maidz why smell cheezbuger nao. **27** Maidz sez littul kitteh coem hoem nao an eatz fudz.

28 Big kitteh sit lukin away frum hooman an wag tail. Kitteh don't want talk to hooman nao. **29** But Big kitteh sez, 'i cant has cheezburgr an i cant has buttsecks, i hatez yu. **30** But you luv littul kitteh an he can haz cheezburger.'

31 'Big kitteh,' teh hooman sed, 'yu iz old. **32** but littul kitteh is kyoot.'"

My kitteh go away an needz fudz an bedz.

Teh Lamp under teh Jar

Luke 18

16 "No wun turnz on teh lamp an den putz it in a bukkit, LOL. He putz teh lamp on teh nietstand so evribodi can see. **17** Evrithin dat is hiddun wil get fownded. **18** If yu haz a lot, yu wil getz moar. If yu duz nawt haff much, you wil evun lose dat, LOL."

Lolrus

John 11

1 In teh hometown uf Mary, thar wuz a dood, LOLrus, who wuz sick. Awl sick liek he ate too much cheezburgerz.

2 You kno, teh Mry who wuz liek, "Happy Cat, ur paws needs to be cleens." But she had no wieps so den she wieps wif her hairs.

3 An teh doods sisturs went to find Happy Cat, an wer liek, "Dis kewl dood is awl sick an stuffz."

4 Happy Cat herd wut dey sed an he wuz awl liek, "Dis is fer teh glory ov Ceiling Cat, cuz I can has glory."

5 Happy Cat lieked teh dood an hiz sisturs.

6 An he totawly tuk his sweet tiem getting reddy, liek two whoel dayz.

7 Den Happy Cat sez, "Road-trip to Judea."

8 But hiz peeps wer awl liek, "O Happy Cat, last tiem we was ther dey wuz totawly nawt kewl."

9 So Happy Cat let dem haff it. "I can has travul by day.

10 If I can has travel at nite, I can has sprained ankul."

11 Happy Cat wuz awl liek "Mah dood Lolrus has naptime. We go, an waek mah dood."

12 But teh peeps were all liek, "If he's nappin dis wud be way eesy."

13 How coem dey no get wut Happy Cat wuz talkin bowt?

14 So Happy Cat no moar tawked wif teh similes an he sed, "Lolrus loozed his bukkit an stuffz.

15 An I am awl glad I wuz not der, but I is heer, so you can beleef. So, lez go."

16 Den teh peep naem Thomas who wuz cawled teh twin, cuz he luks liek Happy Cat, sez, "Yo, lez go to be with teh ded Lolrus an we can be ded awlso."

17 Wen Happy Cat fnally got der he wuz in teh grave for liek three or five dayz.

18 An teh city wuz close to teh hood.

Yu has an emo too!
It's okai, cryin is okay.
**Everywun
can criez.**

19 An lots of doods has caem to tawk to teh sisturs.

20 Den wen dey heer dat Happy Cat wus thar, Martha went to meet dem, but Mary stayed hoem.

21 So Martha saw Happy Cat an sez, "Yu has laet,

22 but I kno Ceiling Cat will totawly lissen to yu."

23 So Happy Cat says, "Your dood will has his bukkit."

24 Martha wus awl liek, "He can't has bukkit in teh ceiling yet."

25 But Happy Cat was all, "No no no, I can has bukkit. An if yu beleev, yu too can has bukkit."

26 "An if yu can has bukkit, yu can has no ded, if yu can has a beleef in Happy Cat. Srsly."

27 Martha den sed, "I can has beleef. An I kno dat yu are teh kitteh of teh Ceiling Cat."

28 So Martha went to her sistur an sed, "Happy Cat aks fer yu." Wich he had nawt.

29 An Mary sez, "Dood!" an ran to Happy Cat.

30 He wuz nawt der yet,

31 but teh doods sez, "Lookit her runnin to pray fer Lolrus."

32 But wen Mary fownded Happy Cat she sez, "Yu has a laet."

33 Den Happy Cat sawed her awl emo an teh Jewkittehs dat coem wif her wer awlso emo an Happy Cat wuz awl sadz an stuffs.

34 "Wer did yu put him?" Happy Cat aksed. "Coem heer an yu can see too," dey sed bac.

35 Happy Cat cry. Nawr jus litle teers, no. He cried big teers. Cuz Lolrus was ded an stufs an everywun luffed him, evun Happy Cat. Happy Cat tried to wiep teers awai wif his pawz but teh teers kept comin an comin an everywun sawed dat as dey were emo too. Everywun was emo. Yeh. Srsly. Yu has an emo too! It's okai, cryin is okay. Everywun can criez. Happy Cat wepted.

36 An teh Jewkittehs saw dis an sed, "See! He wuffs him too!"

37 Den sum ov teh peepul sez, "Diz cat can heel blind catz, can he awlso stop teh Lolrus frum goin to teh ceiling?"

38 An den Happy Cat went to teh tomb an he wuz liek purring, srsly! Teh tomb has stoen in frunt ov teh cave.

39 Happy Cat sez, "Taek awai teh stone! Nao! Kthxbai." But, Martha, LOLrus' sistur sez, "DO NOT WANT! Teh cave iz teh smelli! Lolrus wuz ded four dayz ago!"

40 Den Happy Cat sez, "Iz told yu beefor! If yu beleef, yu can see teh glory of teh Ceiling Cat."

41 So dey moev teh stone. An Happy Cat luk up an sed, "Thanks fer lissenin, Ceiling Cat!

42 Iz kno yu heer me, but dese peeps hangin rownd do nawt beleef in me. Iz show dem."

43 He sed dese tings, den he yelled: "Oh hai! I upgraded ur Lolrus!"

44 Den, Lolrus coem owt. Hiz clothez wuz awl ovur him. An he can nawt see. So Happy Cat sez, "Loose him an let him go nao, kthxbai. Srsly! Nao pls!"

45 Den many catz who coem to Mary saw wat Happy Cat did an beleef.

Happy Cat Goed 2 Jerusalem

Mark 11

1 Wen dey wuz neer Jerusalem an caem to Bethphage an Bethany at teh Mownt of Olivz, Happy Cat sendz 2 of hiz desipulz, **2** an he wuz liek "U goez 2 teh taon ovar dere, an wen yu getz dere yu iz gunna fynd a hors an nobuddy evur roed dat hors. Yu untyz it an bringz it heer, k? 3 An if enywun iz liek 'Hay, wai yu doin dat?' Yu sez 'Teh Lord needz it. Hez gunna bringz it bak wen hez dun.'"

4 An dey went and dey fownd teh hors an it wuz tyd up. An wen dey untyd it, **5** sum peepulz wuz liek "Hay, wai r yu untyin dat hors?" **6** An dey sed wut Happy Cat toldz dem to sai, an teh peepul wuz liek "O, okai!" **7** Wen dey brot teh hors 2 Happy Cat an put deir jackitz on it, Happy Cat satz on it. **8** An lotz of peepul put jackitz on teh rod an othurz put branchiz on teh rod. **9** An teh peepul wuz liek "Yay! Teh gai dat comz in the naem of Ceiling Cat has cheezburgrz! **10** Teh kingdum of David iz gunna hav cheezburgrz! YAY!!!!!"

11 An Happy Cat goed into Jerusalem an went 2 teh tempul, but it wuz laet, so he goed 2 Bethany an goed 2 bed.

12 Teh nekst dai, wen dey wuz leevin Bethany, Happy Cat wuz hungri. **13** He seed teh fud bol an goed 2 see if it hadz fud. But dere wuz no fud, bcuz it wuz not fudz tiem. **14** An Happy Cat wuz liek "OMG yu iz bad fud bol! Nobuddy etz frum yu evar agin!" Srsly.

15 An wen Happy Cat got 2 Jerusalem he goed 2 teh tempul an maed teh peepul sellin an byin stuff leev an he noked ovur all dere stuf, **16** an he wudnt let enywun taek teh stuf dey bot. **17** An he wuz liek "Duznt it sai dat mai hows wil be hows of prair? Yu maed it hows foar bad gaiz!"

18 An evrywun thot taht wuz awsum, but teh preestz an teh

An Happy Cat goed into **Jerusalem** an went 2 teh tempul, but it wuz laet, so he goed.

loyerz wuz liek "OMG! We haz 2 maek him leev!"

19 An wen it wuz all dark an stuf, dey all left teh sitty.

20 In teh mornin, wen dey wuz goinz were dey wuz goinz, dey seed teh fud bol Happy Cat curst an it wuz all durty. **21** An Petur wuz liek "OMG! Teh bol yu curst iz all durty!"

22 An Happy Cat wuz liek "U haz fath in Ceiling Cat, k? **23** If sumwun tellz teh mowntin 2 jumpz in teh see an rly beleevz itz gunna happin, itz gunna happen. **24** So if yu beleevz yu getz wut yu prai foar, den yu getz wut yu prai foar. **25** An wen yu praiz, yu haz to forgiv peepul taht wuz bad 2 u, so Ceiling Cat forgivz u."

27 Dey wuz in Jerusalem agen an wen Happy Cat wuz wawkin in teh tempul, teh preestz an teh loyerz an teh old gaiz caem 2 him. **28** An dey wuz liek "Who sed yu kan do dis stuf?"

29 An Happy Cat wuz liek "Furst yu anserz kwestun foar me, k? **30** Wuz teh likkin cleen of John frum peepul or frum teh Ceiling?"

31 Dey tawked abowt it, an wuz liek "If we sez 'Ceiling,' hez gunna be liek 'Den y didnt yu beleev him?' **32** But if we sez 'peepul,' den all teh peepul iz gunna be mad wif us."

33 An so dey wuz liek "We duznt no!" **34** An Happy Cat wuz liek "Den iz not gunna anser ur kwestun." Srsly

Parable ov teh Two Kittehz

Matthew 21

28 Happy Cat sayed "A naiz hooman had two kittehz. Him sayz to first kitteh, 'good kitteh, yu goes outside nao.' **29** "'DO NOT WANT! iz rainz,' teh kitteh sayz bak. But later is sunni so kitteh goes outside. **30** "Den hooman sayz other kitteh 'yu goes outside nao'. Dis kitteh says, 'okbai'. But dis kitteh don't goed outside, kitteh hides under bed. **31** "Which kitteh iz bestest kitteh?" is Happy Cat trix kwestshun. "wtf dis meanz?" disaiplz askd. Happy Cat sayed, "I sayz srsly, yu is all dum ass, da tax hoomanz, and Romens, and gud jewz, and bad jewz, and fat peepl, and Samariarntans and hookerz are goes up to ceiling before of yuz. srykthnxbai. **32** John showded yu to be good kitteh, and yuz did not want. Da tax hoomanz, and Romens, and gud jewz, and bad jewz, and fat peepl, and cheesemakers, and greeks hookerz dided. And even after yuz saw this, yu still dum ass, srsly."

Teh Last Cheezburger Feest

Mark 14

12 On teh furst day ov teh Feest ov teh Flat Cheezburgers, dey wer gunna maek ded teh moo-cow fer teh dinnur. Teh disiplez ov Happy Cat ask, "Wher do yu want to has cheezburger?" 13 So Happy Cat send two disiplez an he tells dem, "Go to teh citee, yu see a man wif a big bukkit ov wawter. 14 Yu

Dey get reddi fer to big cheezburger feest.

sez to him, 'Teh Smarty Kitteh wan to kno: Whar be mah room so dat I can has cheezburger wif mah disiplez?' **15** He den gunna sho yu tis totawly kewl room wif tabul an stuffz so we can has cheezburgerz."

16 Teh disiplez go an everyfing happuns jus liek Happy Cat sez, cuz he is reely serius an stuffz. Srsly. Dey get reddi fer to big cheezburger feest.

17 Wen it get no liet outsied Happy Cat go to teh kewl room wif his disiplez. **18** Dey wer chillin an restin der pawz an den Happy Cat sez, "I no lie. Wun ov yu gunna tern into bad kitteh an stab me in teh bak. Srsly."

19 Teh disiples awl run owt of happeh, an dey say, "It no me, riet?"

20 "It wun of yu," he sez, "teh wun hoo dip his cheezburger in teh ranch sauwse wif me. **21** Iz gunna be ded jus liek wat writtun in teh buk of Ceiling Cat! Teh kitteh hoo stab me in teh bak totawly gunna wish he no be born!"

22 Wen dey wer nommin Happy Cat taek teh cheezburger an brek it, an he sez, "Taek dis cheezburger an eet it, cuz dis liek mah bodi. But dun reely nom me. Just nom teh cheezburger an pretend it mah bodi. K?"

23 Den he grab teh big cup of booze an gaev tanks to Ceiling Cat, an let dem awl drink frum it (dun worri, noen of dem has cootiez!). Den Happy Cat sez, **24** "Dis mah blud. Teh blud of teh Promis of Ceiling Cat. Yu drink it wif meh. **25** Dis teh las tiem I has booze wif yu guyz, but dun worri, wen I gets to teh Ceiling iz totawly gunna haf booze der."

26 Den dey sang songz an go to teh Mownt Olive to hang owt an luk for mowsies to play wif.

Judas Betrays Happy Cat

Mark 14

32 Den dey went to dis plaec cawled Gethsemane, an Happy Cat sez, "Iz gunna go pray. Stay heer." **33** He tuk Peter, James, an John wif him. Den Happy Cat run owt of Happeh. **34** "Iz a reely sad kitteh. Iz wanna die!" he sez. "Stay heer an wach." **35** He wen a littul furthur away an fawl down, an he want teh tiem to go. **36** "Oh hai Ceiling Cat," Happy Cat praid, "Yu can do anyfing yu want, srsly. Pls dun maek meh do dis."

37 Den he coem bak an he find his disiplez awl takin a cat nap. Den he sez to Peter, "Hey yoo. Simon. Yu stay up an wach owt fer wun hour, k? **38** Pray too, so yu no fawl to temptashunz, srsly. Teh spiritz wantz to do teh riet ting, but teh bodi get in teh way, srsly."

39 Den Happy Cat go bak an pray teh saem ting agin. **40** Wen he got bak he fownd dem takin anudder cat nap. Teh disiplez dunno wat to say to Happy Cat cuz dey cach der own tungs, lol.

41 Den Happy Cat coem an go agin, an he sez, "Doodz, srsly. Did yu liek get no slepe last niet. Enuf! Mah tiem is no moar. Luk, teh sinnars gunna coem an git meh nao. **42** Coem on. Git up, heer coem dat no gud kitteh nao."

43 Den, visible Judas! Wif him he had a bunch of snarlin an meanie kittehs wif weponz an stuffz hoo wer sent by teh top kittehs. **44** Judas say befoar dat he gunna go likk teh wun dey shud put in jael. **45** Goin to Happy Cat he sez, "Teechur!" an gif Happy Cat a likk on teh cheek. **46** Teh men grab Happy Cat an arest him. **47** Den sumwun neerby grab a sword an slash a halpur kitteh of a high preest. No maor eer fer kitteh!

48 "Whai yu coem wif teh weponz? Yu tink I leedin a rebelyon? **49** Everi day I wuz in yer templuz, preechin teh werd, an yu no thro me in jael den. But Ceiling Cat's werd need to be maed tru." **50** Den awl teh kittehs get scaredy an run awai.

Happy Cat on Trial

Mark 15

1 So den awl teh cheefs an kittehs dat rite down teh stuffz haz meetin an tied up teh Happy Cat an taek him to Pilot.

2 An Pilot sez, "Ar yu teh King uv teh Jewkittehs?" An Happy Cat sez bak, "If yu sez so."

3 An teh cheefs wuz in his base, makin akyoosashuns. But Happy Cat relacks an sez nuffin. **4** An Pilot sez to him, "Why yu STFU, dood? Ur gettin pwnd srsly."

5 But teh Happy Cat stil relacks an Pilot wuz liek, "OMFG yu are so leet."

6 See on dis day Pilot gots to let wun uv teh crimnals maek freed. **7** An der wuz a kitteh der naem Barabbas, an he wuz der fer killin soem doodz in teh base. **8** An teh crowdz ask Pilot to maek teh relees liek normul.

9 An Pilot sez, "Shud I maek freed teh King uv teh Jewkittehs?' **10** Cus he kno teh cheefs wuz srsly jellus ov Happy Cat. **11** But teh cheefs sez, "I see wut yu did thar," an maed teh crowdz ask fer Barabbas.

12 An den Pilot sez, "So wat I suppoes to do wif teh King ov teh Jewkittehs?"

13 An teh crowdz sez, "Pwn him!"

14 An Pilot wuz liek, "WTF? Wut he do?" But teh crowdz meow evun lowder: "Pwn him!"

15 An Pilot wantz awl teh peepz to liek him so he maeks free Barabbas an pwns Happy Cat.

Happy Cat on teh Cross

Mark 15

16 Teh soljers led Hapy Cat to teh palass an dey surrownd him. **17** Den dey maed a crown wif thornz an put it on his hed. **18** Den dey cawled owt awl laffin an stuff, "Oh hai. Yu teh King of teh Jews!" **19** Den dey hit him on teh hed lotz of tiems an mokk him an cawl him naemes. Den dey bow down an preten dat they respekt him. Dey awlso spit on him an stuff. **20** Wen dey were dun dey tuk owf teh niec purpul roeb an put Happy Cat's clofes bak on him, an dey leed him awayz to has crusifickshun.

21 An here wus a kitteh frum Cyrene, hoo naem wus Simon, teh faddur ov Alexander an Rufus, wus goin to teh countri an dey wus liek, "Hey yu. Coem heer," an dey maek him to carri teh cross.

22 Den dey bring Happy Cat to teh plaec cawled Golgotha (wich meens Teh Plaec ov teh Skulz). **23** Den dey offur Happy Cat soem booze but he do not want. **24** Den Happy Cat has crusifickshun, an dey rowl diec to see hoo git his clofes.

25 It be teh furd howah wen dey crusify him. **26** An dey put a noet on teh cross dat sez, "KING OV TEH JEWS. LOL" **27** Happy Cat wus nawt teh onlee wun up der. Der wer two robbur kittehs wif him. Wun on teh left an wun on teh riet. **29** Kittehs pass by Happy Cat an dey hiss, maek fun of him, an say bad werds to him. Dey sez, "Yu wus gunna distroy teh tempul an maek it agin in tree dayz huh? **30** Whai yu no coem down an saef yerself if yu so awsum!"

31 Even teh preest kittehs an teh cheef kittehs maek fun of Happy Cat. Dey sez stuff liek,"Oh lookie heer. Happy Cat can maek othur kittehs awl bettah but he no can maek himself bettur. Dat is cuz he is so laem. **32** If Happy Cat coem down frum teh cross den he wud reely be awsum. An we wud has beleef in him. But if he no coem down he is just a silli kitteh an nawt so gret ackshually." Awlso, teh kittehs hoo crusify Happy Cat awlso say meen tings to him.

33 An den it get no liet for tree long hourz, frum teh sicksth hour

Teh Death ov Happy Cat

to teh nienth hour. **34** An den at teh nienth hour Happy Cat yellz owt, "My God, My God! Why have you forsaken me?" which meens in lolspeek, "Oh hai Ceiling Cat. Whai yu leev meh awl aloen?" **35** Soem kittehs neerby heer him an dey tink he is cawling owt to Elijah, cuz dey has bad heering.

36 Wun kitteh ran up to Happy Cat an dip a spunje in nasti booze an put it on a stick so Happy Cat can has drink. But Happy Cat no drink. An anudder kitteh sez,"Leev him aloen nao. Letz see if Elijah coem down an git him."

37 Den Happy Cat run owt of Happy, an he taek his last breth.

38 Oh luk, teh tempul curten rip nao. An no kitteh is maekin it rip! **39** An der wuz dis gard kitteh hoo wus standin neer Happy Cat an heer him cry owt an die, an he goez, "Wow. He mus reely be teh Kitten of Ceiling Cat. Srsly."

40 Sum girl-kittehs wer wachin neerby. Der wus Mary Magdalene, Mary teh mothur of James teh younger an ov Joses, an Salome. **41** Deez kittehs coem an halp Happy Cat in Galilee wen he wus walkin arownd an preechin and stuffz. Der wus awlso lotz of othur girl kittehs hoo coem an see Happy Cat being maed ded.

42 An it wus teh day befor Caturday. It wus gettin no liet owtsied an **43** Joseph of Arimathea, a reel big top cat hoo wus waitin fer teh Ceiling Cat's Ceiling to coem down went to Pilate an sez, "Iz want teh bodi of Happy Cat nao, pleez." **44** Pilate wus liek, "He ded alredy? Srsly?" He acks fer a gard an ask dem if Happy Cat maek ded alredy. **45** Teh gard tel him dat Happy Cat wus alredy maed ded so Pilate gif teh bodi to Joseph. **46** So Joseph get a niec shoebocks an lien it wif niec cloth so dat Happy Cat be all cumfy in der. Deh he put the shoebocks in teh toom an rowl a big huje rok ovur teh door so no kitteh can git in. **47** Mary Magdalene an Mary teh mothur of Joses saw wer he wus put.

Happy Cat Rises from teh Deds

Mark 16

1 So den on Monday Mary Magdalen an Mary hoo wuz James mom taek sum spise to rub on teh Happy Cat bodi so it no stink. **2** An dey getz to teh caev reely erly in teh mornin, liek sunries. **3** An dey wuz wundrin hoo wuz gunna maek teh srsly big rok door opun.

4 An dey luk an seen teh door alredy opun! **5** An wen dey goed in teh caev dey seen a dood thar in wite robes, an dey got skeerd.

6 Teh dood sez, "Oh hai thar, dun be skeerd. yu coem heer lookin fer teh Happy Cat yu lef heer, rite? He caem bak frum teh deds an aint heer no moar. **7** Nao GTFO an tell hiz doodz an Pete an tell em dat dey can haz meetz wif teh Happy Cat in Galilee liek he sed befoer he wuz ded. kthxbi."

8 An teh kitteh leev reely kwik cuz dey was srsly skeerd, an dey dint tawk teh hole way hoem.

9 An teh furst persun teh Happy Cat shode up fer wuz Mary Magdalen. He wunse pwnd sevun demunz dat wuz livin in her harbls. **10** An she told hiz doodz abowt her meetz an dey maed a cry. **11** Wen dey tink abowt teh Happy Cat seein Mary an not dem, dey stard tinkin, "No wai. He stil ded."

12 Den teh Happy Cat apeerd to two moar uv his doodz wile dey out taekin a wawk. **13** Dey told teh udder doodz bowt it but dey sez, "No wai."

14 So den Happy Cat showed up to awl his doodz wile dey was hafin teh cheezbergurs an yelt an pwnd dem fer not baleevin he wuznt ded no moar.

15 An he sez, "GTFO an tell all teh cats an kittehs on Urfs

Oh hai thar, dun be skeerd. yu coem heer lookin fer teh Happy Cat yu lef heer, rite?

abowt meh. **16** Tell dem teh cats dat beleev an ar dunkd ar full of WIN, an teh wuns dat dont ar on teh FAILBOAT an gunna get pwnd in teh Basement. **17** An teh peepz full of WIN getz mah levul ups an gonna be abul to pwn demuns, **18** an junghul snaeks, an drank poysin wifowt gittin hert, an maek kittehs no moar ded. Kthnxbai."

19 An wen he wuz doen talkin wif dem he taek INVISIBLE EVEVATER to teh Ceiling an sat at da rite paw of Ceiling Cat. **20** An dey went an teld awl teh kittehs wut happun, an Ceiling Cat halp dem do amazun stuffz to proev it. Kthxbai.

Pennycots

Acts 2

1 Wen teh dai of teh Pennycots cam, dey wer togedder in wun plaec.

2 Den, holy moos, a sawnd lyk many kittehs yellin "MIAO!" cam frum teh ceiling and filld teh hawse wher teh d00ds wuz chillin.

3 Dey sawd lickys of fyre dat cam ovr ther heds and omg it burnz! it burnz! Oh wait, no it dont!

4 All of them d00ds wuz feelin' teh Hover Cat,an dey all talkd in stranj LOLspeek lik: "I do say sir, what have we got here? I do believe there are tongues of fire-like substance coming upon our heads. and making us speak in quite the funniest way." WTF iz wif dat? Cuz teh Hover Cat maed it happun, w00t!

5 Now teh d00ds wuz chillin in Jerooslum, Joos who feerd teh Ceiling Cat, frum evry nashun undur teh Ceiling, srsly.

6 Wen dey herd da sawnd, a litter caym and wer lyk, "No Wai!" cuz dey all talkd in weerd LOLspeeks.

7 Wow'd fer shur, dey axed,"Arnt deez teh d00ds who speekd Gallyleen bfor, watz happnin?

8 Den haw duz we heerz our naytiv LOLspeeks? Srsly!"

9 Angoras, an Manxs an Tabbies; an kittehs frum Persia an Abyssinia,

10 an Ejipt an teh partz of teh Burma neer Siam. Der were also kittehs frum resurch labz!

11 both teh Joos and da switchies two Joodyizm frum teh feilds an aleewaiz, herd dem,"we heer dem myowin' teh 1ders ov teh Ceiling Cat in aur LOLspeeks!" WTF?

12 Wow'd and confoozd dey sez, "WAI DO THEY SPEEK DIS WAY?!?! WAI?"

13 And sum peepl laffed at dem and sed:"Ya, rite. Dey nom too much gatorade, Srsly."Don wurry, Ceiling Cat pwnz dem peepl latur. Kthx.

"Ya, rite. Dey nom too much gatorade, Srsly."

42 Den dey gotz cookiez an dey praid and lissen to teh oder kittehs **43** Everywun wuz all happeh and teh apawsles didz a majic sho, srsly. **44** An dey wer all frenz, lol. **45** Dey sell stuffz like blanketz and oder stuffz, an dey giv stufz to poor kittehz.

46 Evewy day dey met an went an had sleep ovahs and slumbah partayz an dey eated cookiez! **47** Dey worshipz Ceiling Cat an den he wuz all happeh an teh apawsles can has moar saveded kittehs!

Saul on teh Damascus Road

Acts 9

1 At saemtiem Saul still wuz sayin bad stufs aganst Ceiling Cat's discipuls. He goed to high preest **2** He ask teh high preest for ledderz to teh sinamagogz in Damascus, so if he foundz ani menz or womenz who follow Ceiling Cat, he could taek dem an puts in Jerusalem jale. **3** As he wuz on teh way to Damascus, all of suddens lite appear! Lite frum Ceiling, zomg! **4** Saul gotz skeerd so he fells to ground and Ceiling Cat speekz. "Saul, wtf, why yu hurtz me?"

5 "Who is u?", Saul asks.

6 Ceiling Cat sez, "I iz Happy Cat, ftw! And yu iz hurting me an my peeps. Yu must go to teh city, yu will getz instrukshunz der."

7 Teh othur guiz Saul waz travlins wif wif were like, "Um k, wtf?", cuz they hurd Ceiling Cat but din't see Him. **8** Saul got up from teh grownd but he reelize that he culdn't see nuthing cuz crazie lite maed him blind. So teh othur guiz helped Saul gets rest of wai to Damascus. **9** Saul blind fer three days, an during dese days he not drink or eats foodz. Not even cheezburger!

10 In Damascus der waz discipul by naem of Ananias. Ceiling Cat spoek to him in vishun. Ananias anserd an sed, "Oh hai! What up?"

11 Ceiling Cat sed, "Der is howse of Judas on Straight Street. Yu mus goes cuz ther man from Tarsus naemd Saul, and he iz prayin. **12** I shoewd him vishun, and in vishun you putted your paws on him and gif him back his site."

13 Ananias anserd. "But I has heards stuff bout this gui. Isn't he dat guy who was pwning your saintz an stuff? **14** And he haz comes here with cheef preestz athority to putz your peeps in jale! Iz I not rite?"

15 Ceiling Cat says "Yes, he waz but he differn now. I has maded him to followz me an speak in my naem to teh Gentiles, ther kingz and Israel peeps. **16** I shoewz him how much he mus suffur for mah name. No worriez, kk?"

17 So Ananias wented to howse. He foundz Saul and dids wut Ceiling Cat say. He place paws on Saul. Ananias sed, "Hai Saul, Ceiling Cat, who pwnded your eyez with crazie lite, sented me to yu so you cans be filld with teh Hover Cat. kk? You can has site bak." **18** Then weerd scaly thingz fell frum Saul's eyes. Saul seez again, ftw!!! Furst thing he do: he getz baptisd. **19** Then he eated fudzstufs cuz he wuz hungry. Fud maded him strongur!

26 Saul wented bak to Jerusalem, an he tryd to join teh discipuls der, cept they were like "OMG" cuz they dunt beleeve he camez to be Ceiling Cat's discipul. **27** But Barnabas talkd with the discipuls an tolded them all abowt how Saul camez to be Ceiling Cat's discipul too cuz of teh crazie lite on teh wai to Damascus. **28** So the dicipuls beleeved Barnabas, and tehy let Saul stai wif dem. Togedder tehy preeched teh Gospel in Jerusalem, in teh name of Ceiling Cat! **29** Tehn Saul preeched to Grecian Jews. They were like "Diz guy needs a gud pwning. He iz not of Ceiling Cat!" **30** Teh other discipuls herd this, so tehy taeks Saul to Caesarea and sended him to Tarsus, away from crazi ppl.

As he wuz on teh way to Damascus, all of suddens lite appear! Lite frum Ceiling, zomg!

Ceiling Cat Prayer

Teh Ceiling Cat of us, whu haz cheezeburger, yu be spechul
Yu ordered cheezburgerz,
Wut yu want, yu gets, srsly.
In ceiling and on teh flor.

Giv us dis day our dalee cheezburger.
And furgiv us for makin yu a cookie, but eateding it.
And we furgiv wen cats steel our cookiez.

An do not let us leed into teh showa,
but deliver us from teh wawter.
Ceiling Cat pwns all. He pwns teh ceiling and teh floor
and walls too.

Forevur and evuhr.
Amen.

Amayzin Grase

Amayzin grase, how niec yu soundz
Yu saevded a bad kitteh liek me!
I wunse gets lost but nao ai fowndz!
oh hai, nao can ai see!

Teh grase, maeded mah hartz awl sceerd.
Teh grase, yu maek it all bettah.
Hao niec teh Grase be awl appeerd.
Wen ai be a niec kittah.

Thru big vaccume, loud dogz, an snaekes
Iz not gunna be ded
Dat grase bringded meh, it no liek taekes
an it gif me a big cumfy bed

Ceiling Cat beez bery gud to meh
He be alwais reely so coo
He kepe me saef even if dey betteh
He neva trete me liek a ful

Wen mah nien lifes be all teh goen
Wen ai gif mah last wun upz
Iz gunna go teh Ceiling, an dat gunna pwn
All teh catnip an no pups!

Amayzin grase, how niec yu soundz
Yu saevded a bad kitteh liek me!
I wunse gets lost but nao ai fowndz!
oh hai, nao can ai see!

Awl Fings Brite an Purtyful

All fings brite an purtyful,
All kittehs big an small,
All fings wize an wunnerful,
Ceiling Cat mekked dem all.

Teh teeny flowurs dat open,
Teh burds an flying fings,
He mekked ther tasty gudness,
He mekked ther teeny wings.
All fings brite ...

Teh hoomans wiv big howses,
Teh ones livin on teh street,
Dey has difrent siez burgers,
But all can stil has eats.
All fings brite ...

Teh big hills an teh mountins,
Teh deep sea an teh ground,
Teh Lolrus an his bukkit,
Dat nevar wil be found
All fings brite ...

Teh chilly winz in wintar,
Teh niec wawm summy sun,
Teh ripe noms an teh catnip,
He mekked dem evry wun.
All fings brite ...

Teh Caturdays iz win-ful,
He mekked Cat Monorail,
He mekked teh lolz an capshuns,
Wivout dem we has a Fail .
All fings brite ...

Dees fings iz not invisible,
Cos He givved us eyez to see,
Epic Ceiling Cat iz Epic,
Cos He invntd ICHC!
All fings brite ...

Argooments fer Ceiling Cat

Pascal's Wayjjur

Pascal wus clever kitteh hu wus laik: "I am not knoin if teh Ceiling Cat is reel." Oh noes! But Pascal was thinkin an thinkin, an he wus laik "If I is beleefin in teh Ceiling Cat, and he is reel, I will be gettin cheezburger. But if I has no beleefin in teh Ceiling Cat, and he is reel, I will be getting pwned. If there no Ceiling Cat, no matter anywai. I think I is beleefin in teh Ceiling Cat."

Fiwst Cawse

Evewythin need a cawse, cuz, um, dat is how it is. We mew an hoomins gif us fud. Hoomins go in noysy box an go awayz an dey com bak wif fud. Dis is cawse an effekt. Who gifs teh hoomins fud? Oder hoomins cant gif hoomins fud so Ceiling Cat mus be givin dem fud for us and dem. See, Ceiling Cat bless teh hoomins wif fud for feedin us, how niec of Ceiling Cat! Hoomins must be pettin him awl teh tiem!

Ceiling Cat maed teh fiwst mew, an he maed fud for awl hoomins and kittehs. Der be no utta way to maek fud, srsly. So Ceiling Cat stawteded it awl!

Felinopik Prinsipul

Teh howse is jus riet for us kittehs. Is not too cowd or too hot. Is jus niec an warm an cuddlee. Teh hoomins gif us fud wen we ask an scrach us wen we mew qyoot. We gets to slepe anywhar an teh hoomins even gif us warm piels of cleen close to lay on. How awesoem!

If Ceiling Cat dint ecksist how cud all of dis happun? If teh howse wus too cowd we wud be ded kittehs wif ice! If teh howse wus too hot we wud be ded kittehs wif crispees! If hoomins not der to feed us we wud be reely skinneh and ded kittehs. If Ceiling Cat dint maek hoomins for us sleepin anywhar wud not be fun! An no cleen close to slepe on!

Evewythin in howse is riet for kitteh and dat is how we kno Ceiling Cat is reel, srsly.

Wen in teh Ceiling...

- kittehs can has scratches on teh cowches awl dey want. No hoomans trai an stop dem. An teh foam, it has a flavur.

- kittehs can has a bag to plai wif anytiem dey want. In fact, in teh Ceiling, yu alwais heer teh soft russul of bagz.

- kittehs can has petz awl teh tiem. Wenever dey want. An der is alwais a window dat dey can luk owt ov.

- kittehs can has sunbeemz wenevur dey want. Srsly. Kittehs in teh Ceiling alwais warm.

- kittehs can akshually cach teh laser beemz. Srsly. Dey taist reely gud.

- kittehs can has wet fud awl teh tiem. Srsly. An it dunt maek der breff stink!

- Kittehs can has Caturday everiday!

About the LOLCat Bible

The question I get asked a lot is, "Why did you start the LOLCat Bible Translation Project?" I sometimes stumble a bit with a clear answer because for me, creating the site was a simple leap of faith. What I can say is that the LOLCat Bible teaches a lesson about running with an idea.

When I formed the LOLCat Bible website in July of 2007, I honestly didn't expect too much to come out of it, except perhaps some people stopping by to view the curiosity and contribute a bit. Instead I was greeted with an outpouring of suggestions, discussions, and translations. The site, www.lolcatbible.com, was about to become larger than I ever expected.

This book stands as a testament to the work that has been done from all corners of the world. I would like to give a very special thanks to the user Anshkakashi, who did a wonderful job in the early stages of the LOLCat Bible Translation Project. I would also like to thank all the project's contributors for their inspirational, and funny, translations. Without all of you, the project would have not been as successful as it has been. This is by no means an exhaustive list of the over 2000 members who each gave a contribution, whether one verse or several chapters. The following people have been very helpful and have done a large portion of the total work: Superiority, Proculus, Jedi, Cattus petasatus, Medicat, Simon w, Joaquin67, Omegainstigator, Billlol, D1ppyd0g D, jkatscan, Atheist, Pseudonym, Vlad the Impala, Bboyneko, SDCat, Chelseaneko, Raevis, Ragesoss, Dial mcat, Sips, Diminati, Cwoozy, Forestcat, Landei, Risser, MattieBoi11, Masterbratac, Zenkitty, 3moose1.

What's amazing is that the LOLCat Bible Translation Project is still not finished. In fact, you can still login to the site and modify the text and contribute. There are even some portions of the Bible that have no translation yet, waiting for someone with that spark of creativity to fill them in. After all, Ceiling Cat would want you to improve the site and help translate the Bible so he can bestow upon you a multitude of cheeseburgers and cookies. Srsly.

—Martin Grondin